THE ART AND CRAFT

of Entertaining

THE ART AND CRAFT

of Entertaining

KIMBERLY KENNEDY

ATRIA BOOKS

New York   London   Toronto   Sydney

ATRIA BOOKS
1230 Avenue of the Americas
New York, NY 10020

Photography © Wendell T. Webber
Design: Julian Peploe
Project management services: Paula Litzky
Text services: Victoria Spencer
Food stylist: Toni Brogan
Prop stylist: Renata Chaplynsky

ISBN-13: 978-0-7432-7835-5
ISBN-10:   0-7432-7835-6

First Atria Books hardcover edition November 2005

10   9   8   7   6   5   4   3   2   1

ATRIA BOOKS is a trademark of Simon & Schuster, Inc.

For information regarding special discounts for bulk purchases,
please contact Simon & Schuster Special Sales at 1-800-456-6798
or business@simonandschuster.com

Manufactured in the United States of America

TO TODD—

MY HUSBAND AND BEST FRIEND

ACKNOWLEDGMENTS

I am so grateful for the opportunities that have been given to me. I would like to personally thank those that helped make this book a reality. Without their artistry, diligence, encouragement, and multiple kindnesses, the road would have been a steeper climb.

For all that I have been given, I appreciate and thank . . .

Simon and Schuster, Atria Books, and the rest of my creative team:

Brenda Copeland, for her belief in this project, endless energy, and positive attitude.

Judith Curr, for giving this book all that it needed to become its very best.

Paula Litzky, for truly listening, understanding me, and assembling a team that perfectly captured my vision for this book.

Victoria Spencer, for working tirelessly and finding my voice when I sometimes felt there was nothing left.

Julian Peploe, for having a keen sense for design and pulling it all together.

Wendell T. Webber, for capturing and bringing everything to life so exquisitely.

Amy Tannenbaum, for keeping us young by adding a much-needed perspective.

Renata Chaplynsky, for making everything she touched beautifully stylish.

Toni Brogan, for feeding our eyes with her superb presentations.

Kevin Goon, for his long hours spent organizing all the details.

Nicole Bryl, for being my personal cheerleader and always making me look good.

Ana Hsu, for keeping everything in good measure.

Gail Nguyen, for, quite honestly, saving the day.

The people who started it all:

Eric Schotz, Bill Paolantonio, Laurie Girion, Robin Kass, Bonnie Clark, and CBS, for finding this homemaker from the South and giving me a chance to follow a dream.

My agent:

Jason Hodes and the William Morris Agency, for agreeing to join me on this adventure and help guide me on my path.

To all of those who have supported me through the years and enriched my life with their friendship, I wish to thank . . .

My husband, Todd Kennedy, for allowing me to pursue my interests and encouraging and supporting me in all my personal endeavors. He deserves recognition for loving me despite my imperfections and for being unbelievably understanding and patient. My life is so much more beautiful with his kindness and adorable smile in it.

Both of my parents for giving me confidence and encouragement to follow my passions:
My mother, Cyndy Hartman, for introducing me to, and sharing her love for, all things domestic. I learned from her example what being a gracious hostess truly means. In addition to teaching me so much, she is always willing to give a helping hand. I want to thank her for always being there for me.

My father, Paul Hartman, for teaching me the importance of continued education and using acquired knowledge to accomplish my dreams. I want to thank him for building my first play kitchen, for always giving sound advice, and for believing that I could accomplish anything I set out to do.

My friends:
Dawn Schedule, for all of her hard work and enthusiasm—this experience would not be the same without it. This has been a great journey, but the best part was finding her for a friend.

Kara, Drennen, Ashley, Amy, Andrea, Caroline, Kristen, and Kim, for their friendship and support, especially over the past year. It has meant more to me than they will ever know.

Nicholas Kniel and Timothy Wright, for their unending generosity, advice, and friendship.

Gary Shapiro and Katy McCaffrey, for (quite possibly) providing the spark that lit the fire. Here's to mojitos, long days in the sun, and never having to move your own umbrella.

Bobby Flay, for believing in me, giving me direction, and never judging me as I learn the ropes.

My little dog Sadie, for loving me unconditionally and always bringing a smile to my face.

My inspiration, Julia Child, a friend I never got the chance to personally meet—she had a wonderful ability to teach without ever making me feel like a student.

Contents

Introduction

Having a good time, that's what it's really all about. Actually, entertaining is perhaps about creating as well as enjoying a good time, about making special memories for you and your friends and guests.

This book was born out of my love of entertaining. Many people find that very word "entertaining" intimidating. Gathering friends and family at your place to enjoy good food and good company sounds so appealing, but the idea of planning the party, cleaning the house, making the food, and playing hostess seems so stressful and time-consuming. Over the years, friends have turned to me because they want to entertain but don't know where to start. I realized that despite the plethora of glossy entertaining tomes on bookstore shelves, there was room for mine. A book that tells you how you can do it but doesn't demand you copy my style. A book full of information and inspirations that will start you on the path to entertaining savvy or, if you are already a seasoned hostess, can provide fresh inspiration for the parties to come.

I believe that entertaining can be empowering. Pulling off an enjoyable party is something to be proud of. You should feel good that you can plan, organize, and execute a successful event, that you can entertain in your own inimitable style. Be guided by the information in this book, take some of the ideas and marry them with your own, and you'll be on the way to developing your style and gaining confidence as a hostess and elsewhere in your life. Take pride in what you do and how you do it.

I really relish making all kinds of things, from invitations to decorations, to gifts and stylish binders and inspiration boards that encourage my creativity and help me to be organized when planning a party. My love of sewing, cooking, and entertaining comes from my mother. When I was growing up, my parents invited friends over regularly, and my mom always enjoyed setting an elegant table and serving interesting and delicious food. I am lucky to have had such a great example to follow. My mom says that when I was small she was determined to interest me in crafting, but there were not many craft stores back then (in the late seventies!).

She did manage to find a large art store across town and we would make weekly trips to pick out the "craft of the week." Usually that meant a hook latch rug, pom-pom animals, jewelry supplies, or a doll-making kit. I would get lost for hours within the aisles of Treasure Island, always eager to try my little hands at every possible craft. By the time I was five, I had my first sewing machine (a children's hand-crank model), and my dad was letting me help in his woodshop. That's where my interest in woodworking started.

Now I'm lucky enough to have a very practical spouse; Todd and I built our first home together and he is a constant inspiration to me, urging me to try different tools and techniques, to give it a shot.

I want to encourage you to try this approach. Not everything works the first time, but as some old sage said, we learn by our mistakes. I've found that it's possible to learn a lot along the way; as you try new projects and recipes, plan bigger or more sophisticated parties, there is much fun to be had. I realize that not everyone wants to make everything from scratch or has the time to do so, so this book is an à la carte offering. Take from it what you can use and build on it in your own unique way. Give it a go and let me be your guide to stylish entertaining.

CHAPTER I

A *Question* of STYLE

Style is one of life's intangibles: easy to recognize, but harder to define. We may know who's got it. But can we say for sure what it is?

Style is comprised of our likes and dislikes. It finds a voice in what we wear and what we surround ourselves with, but it's more than just the outward appearance of our preferences. Style is an expression of the way we move through life. It marks our attitudes and communicates our desires and is reflected in everything we do, from the homes we choose, to the clothes we wear, the books we read, the music we listen to—and of course, the way we entertain.

Your style is unique to you. At least it should be. You might think that you dress a lot like a dear friend, but look closely and you'll find subtle and significant differences. Style is about expression, not imitation, and it's *not*

Style is an expression of the way you move through life.

the same as fashion. Style has nothing to do with being thin, young, rich, or beautiful. And like beauty, it's much more than skin deep. Style is not just about personal appearance or how your home looks, it really does reflect every aspect of life, including entertaining. Say you prefer casual to formal; that's a matter of style and it will reflect the way you entertain. If you choose time-honored recipes or like to experiment with the latest fusion food, that also indicates your style and inspires your entertaining. I love to entertain and realize that my desire to share good times with friends—that's the heart of entertaining—has grown as I've come to a place where I am sure of my style. Knowing what I like has given me confidence to express myself and share my style with others.

MY STYLE . . .

I'd describe my style as traditional and sophisticated, with a sassy twist. I don't care for anything stuffy or too crazy, but I do like fun things and will use them with classic pieces. That's true of how I dress and how I entertain. For example, I love Burberry. It's traditional and proper—and very well made. They've been in business for more than 150 years, so you know they must be doing something

right. Even so, I'd never do a whole head-to-toe look. That would be too extreme, and just not me. So I'll wear a pair of jeans and a favorite white shirt with a Burberry scarf tied round my waist and maybe a stylish pair of boots. That way I can take what's timeless, blend it with what's fashionable, and come up with my own trademark.

. . . AND HOW I GOT HERE

As a kid I looked pretty much like the friends I hung out with: kind of preppy, lots of polo tops and khakis, a couple of flowery dresses. Then in college I lost interest in how things looked. I was busy studying and enjoying the freedom of being away from home and style just wasn't that important to me. I had a uniform of jeans, fleece tops, and hiking boots. (Maybe it was so that I could blend in with all the guys I hung out with?)

After college that all changed. By then I'd moved to Atlanta and was spending time with friends who had terrific style and clothing sense. Next to them, I looked, well, boring. So I started to pay more attention to what I wore. At the same time I got my first apartment, a tiny rented place. I had no furniture and virtually no cash. Sound familiar? Even so, I don't know what made me decorate it

Style is the dress of thought.

THE EARL OF CHESTERFIELD

the way I did, all stark black and white. Maybe it was a way of making an asset of my lack of possessions. Looking back it's amazing that I lived with that look for three years, but at the time I really did like it. After that experiment I realized that I'm not the minimalist type. I understood that after I got married and Todd and I moved into our first house. A whole house! It was so exciting, I couldn't wait to use different colors and textures to escape from the black and white prison I'd created for myself. I sold all the stuff from my old apartment at a yard sale and—faster than you can say *French provincial*—went from that "put your stereo on a pedestal" kind of look to a "hide your TV in a country French armoire" kind of look. My style has evolved over time. I'm really comfortable with myself and my tastes now, with who and how I am—and how the world sees me.

CIRCLE OF FRIENDS

When you're in high school, even college, there's a definite sense that you should be like, look like, and sometimes even think like the people you hang out with. Thankfully that doesn't last forever. Today, my friends and I are still close—we still have a lot in common—but we've gone our separate ways when it comes to style.

Ashley is a fine artist who always makes a splash. Talented and expressive, her passion for art and for life is apparent in the way she talks, dresses, and decorates her home. Her place has a lot of different artwork and blends all kinds of old and unique furniture. Her clothes are funky, like her artwork: vibrant colors, crazy shoes, and often splotches of paint "decorate" her outfits. I don't think Ashley owns any china or crystal, her tableware being an eclectic mix of bold and bright pieces.

Caroline is quite different. She's tiny and quiet, with a style that is simple and clean. She's more traditional than I am and chooses calm, neutral colors for both her wardrobe and her home. Her house is neat and functional and not at all fussy. Her clothes are simple and elegant, and she keeps accessories to a minimum, usually her favorite pearl earrings. Caroline has lovely traditional silver and crystal and a very classic china pattern, one that's been popular for the last fifty years.

FINDING YOUR STYLE

Discovering and even defining your style is a lot easier than you realize. Think about what you like to wear. What colors, what patterns (if any) do you adore? Do you prefer cowboy boots or stilettos? Do you wear those cowboy boots with jeans or long flowing dresses? Do you like beaded purses or prefer a functional backpack? Think of a friend's house that you love. What elements speak to you? Is it the dreamy porch with a swing or the gleaming professional-style kitchen range? Or maybe it's the couch in that glorious blue-green color? Do you like lots of textures on a table or lots of color or both? What makes you comfortable, happy, and contented? Is it certain colors, certain fabrics, or maybe particular foods? Making a list of ten (or twenty!) things that really speak to you, not necessarily things you own or aspire to buy, just things, rooms, colors that strike a chord can help to define your style.

Some of my very favorite things are priceless, my Yorkshire terrier Sadie for one. Some are pricey like the Waterford crystal vases. I love how crystal reflects the light. The little cherub—I don't know why I like it but I do—I don't know how old the statue is or where it was made. Originally I bought it to go in the garden but then I liked it so much I wanted to keep it in the house and I do like the idea of bringing things meant for the outdoors in. My favorite perfume is from Jo Malone, I wear it all the time; what might be more suprising is that I love the bottle as much as the fragrance! The shape, the stopper, they appeal to my eye. I even love the way they wrap the perfume and the bags are to die for. But then some of the other things I adore don't really have much of a price tag. My favorite colors are blues, all kind of robins-egg–like shades, and browns, rich warm tones of brown. I particularly love combining these two colors in the trim on projects, on the table, even my business card. Silk is my fabric of choice; I use it a lot in decorating my home and love to use it for crafty projects. There are so many gorgeous shades of silk at the fabric store that I can't resist. And ribbon, well I'm crazy about ribbon; I make entire projects with ribbon and use it to trim just about everything I make or wrap as a gift or favor.

If someone asked me what flower I like best, I'd say hydrangea. It's by far the flower I buy most to have at home, just to look at and admire—blue, white, pink—I think they're all gorgeous.

Take it a step further. Whom do you admire—and why? The women I admire for their style of dress are true icons: Coco Chanel, Jackie Kennedy, Audrey Hepburn. They have a sophisticated yet clean look that I aspire to. I'm also in awe of how polished they were, and I've come to realize that this is not because they were fashionable, but because they had an understanding of themselves that gave them confidence. Above all, they were comfortable in their own skin. Turning in a different direction, I also look up to Julia Child. She was so wonderfully lively and nonplussed—even when her food hit the deck on live TV. You've got to give her points for that.

Identifying the people you look to for inspiration should give you clues as to the nature of your style. But you don't have to do it all on your own. Ask your friends how they would describe your style. They can have great insights into what makes you tick. You might not agree with what they say but it will be informative. Haven't you ever been shopping with a friend when she picks out something that's perfect for you but you'd gone right past it?

Fashion changes with what's going on around you.
Style changes with what's
going on in you. CATHERINE PATTISON

THE SUBSTANCE OF STYLE

I'm not going to try to pinpoint every available style; it's just not possible. I do want to outline some of the basic style groups to help you enhance your own. I doubt you're going to fit into exactly one of them. Frankly, I don't know anyone who is totally country casual or entirely urban chic. Most of us like a little bit of this, a lot of that, and quite a bit of something else too! In fact I'd say the biggest style today is mix and match, kind of a buffet approach where people feel free to take what they like from one look and mix it up with something totally different.

Bear in mind that these styles cover a wide swath of territory; for me some country styles are it, but there are others that come under the country umbrella that I never like. Style is a big store and you don't have to do all your shopping in one department!

CASUAL COUNTRY Everything from traditional country (*Little House on the Prairie*–type small floral fabrics, lace) to French Country (think lavender and soft linens) to Americana (think denim, bandanas, lots of leather). Generally country means relaxed, casual, and well worn—or at least looking like it is well worn. A country table might have a tablecloth with big roses, cream polka dot plates, and big wooden bowls.

TIME-HONORED TRADITIONAL The more buttoned-down cousin of country. Think oxford shirts and twin sets, or polished wood furniture in classic styles, wingback armchairs, and a table set with "proper" matching china, flatware, and crystal.

MOD MINIMAL A strong streamlined look, think black and chrome furniture and all black clothes with one strong accessory. To achieve this pared-down style you need a lot of closet space! A table would be set with oversized wineglasses, square plates, bold plain silverware, and plain linen napkins. It's all in the line, not the decoration.

URBAN CHIC Like traditional, this is a neat and uncluttered style but much more contemporary. It's hip and more colorful than mod minimal, also a bit funkier, looser. You don't have to live in the city to like this one! Imagine green and black Japanese bowls set atop oversized terracotta chargers and you're halfway there.

ABSOLUTELY ECLECTIC A wild mix of colors, patterns, and pieces. Eclectic means "made up of elements from various sources," so this is a think-outside-the-box kind of style: a dentist's chair in the middle of the living room, the sharp black designer suit with a ruffled blouse and tons of antique costume jewelry. For entertaining, picture Grandma's china with dollar-store tumblers and dishcloth napkins. If you can't define something another way, call it eclectic!

CONTEMPORARY A super-comfy neutral look that's contemporary but easy-going. It's a great background look that blends well with other styles. The palette is cream, taupe, and white, often with accents of bold or dark colors. It travels from the beach to the city. Grown up but not stuffy, it's the kind of things you find at Pottery Barn or Crate & Barrel. It's the latest style of cargo pants paired with a slim-fitting tee.

project STYLE FILE

Creating a style file where you can collect images and inspirational materials and keep them together in one place where you can be sure to find them can be fun and practical. I have kept a style file for about ten or eleven years now, although I did not always call it that. It was just my notebook. I began quite simply by pulling pictures I liked from magazines. I like to organize, so I decided to take things up a notch and get those neat see-through sleeves. As I was sticking the pages into the sleeves, I began categorizing them so they'd be easier to flip through. Before I knew it, I had this huge three-inch binder, though I still called it my notebook. I took it with me when I was shopping in a fabric warehouse, and when I checked out they tried to give me the decorator discount. The lady explained that I was carrying a style file like all the decorators do, so she'd assumed I was a decorator. When I explained that I wasn't a decorator I didn't get the discount, but I did learn that I had a style file!

Over the years the look of my style file has changed. Now it has a beautiful cover and a divider system. I love to flip through my file for both inspiration and information. I use it for everything from entertaining to decorating and sometimes just to browse when I have a spare moment.

Organize your style file in the way that's best for you. Mine contains a lot of information about my house, with a slide sheet page at the front holding paint chips from each room. Then there is a section for each room, complete with the dimensions and fabric swatches from existing furniture and drapes. There's a section for landscaping, one for window treatments, and a gift section where I keep ideas for homemade gifts and giftwrap ideas. The very last section is for contacts, it's a zippered pouch where I keep brochures and business cards and other vital contact information.

What I keep in my style file is pretty varied. Pages from home, lifestyle, food, and fashion magazines can be found there plus images from catalogs. I might pull something from a fashion magazine, a bag, say, not because I want to buy that bag but because I love the closure and want to make a pouch with that kind of closure as a gift. I'll take an image of a tall cupboard because I'm looking for something kind of like that and don't know how to describe it—sometimes showing a salesperson a picture really is worth a thousand words. I might tear out an image of a home in another country, not because I'm going to decorate my great room just like that but because I really like how the blue shades are combined in that Moroccan room, and that may end up informing the table for a party I host. Start a style file as a means of exploring what you like and a concrete way to reference your tastes. Keep building your style file, adding images and information because as it grows it will be an ongoing, practical guide to your style.

PULLING IT ALL TOGETHER

A lot of people I know have a hard time defining their style. This prevents them from entertaining because, as they are not confident of who they are, they cannot be confident that what they do and present to others—the food, the table, the atmosphere of the party—will be "right." Often people say they don't entertain because they don't have a dining table, their place is too small, they can't cook well enough, or there isn't enough time. Really though it comes down to confidence and this relates to knowing yourself, your style. Everything comes easier when you have a concrete understanding of what you like, what your look is, and how you share your style with those around you. Style is an expression of you. So getting to know your style is a great first step to hosting a party. Once you know your style, everything you do and the choices you make—selecting the gift you give, deciding on the menu for a dinner party or how to decorate a room—will come more easily. If you serve dishes that you find delicious, set the table so you find it attractive, then you will be less stressed and your guests will be more comfortable. Personal style does not suddenly appear, it evolves over time, but starting to think about your preferences now will help you to develop your style, and others will begin to recognize your "look," your own trademark style.

CHAPTER 2

Best Laid PLANS

Entertaining has long been a part of my life, but it wasn't always about cocktail parties and sit-down dinners for eight. When I was a little girl I would have tea parties for my dolls and my friends. Since I wasn't a sugar and spice sort of child, my tea parties would be held in my tree fort. I'd serve pretend pies made of backyard berries, flowers, leaves, and, of course, dirt made in my Easy-Bake Oven pans. I didn't plan my parties then, which is why sometimes I wouldn't have enough berry pies to feed all my guests. Oh well, live and learn.

My love of entertaining and parties comes from my mom—she has always been such an inspiration to me. My dad too. From them I've learned the joy of entertaining, of how sharing and giving to others can enrich all of our lives, bringing joy to family and friends in good measure.

When I was growing up we constantly had guests—for dinner, for the holidays, for all kinds of occasions, and sometimes for no occasion at all. Entertaining seemed to come naturally to my parents; in fact, we didn't think of it as entertaining. It was just having family and friends over, for good meals and good times. Not until later did I find out their secret, that being organized and planning ahead allowed them not just to throw these wonderful parties, but to be able to join in and enjoy themselves as much as their guests did.

I guess you could say that I learned by example. That's not true for everyone, though. I've met many wonderful cooks and hostesses who either taught themselves or went

THE PROMISE OF PLANNING

The importance of planning and organizing was made clear to me one day when, after a pleasant summer evening spent with friends, one of my guests pulled me aside: "Honestly," she said. "I don't know how you do it!" I laughed. Her tone was so reverential—she seemed so impressed—that I thought she was joking, that next she was going to ask me what kind of laundry detergent I used. She went on: "Really, this all looks like it comes straight from one of those entertaining books you're always reading. I could never pull this off." It was then I realized she was serious.

I was flattered, of course. Who wouldn't be? It's always

It takes as much energy to wish

to cooking school. Their desire to cook and entertain was sort of a reaction to the TV dinners or sometimes hurried meals they grew up eating at home. Dinner guests were rare for them, so now they host dinner parties all the time, taking pride in experimenting with menus and table settings, even their selection of the evening's music. All this is to say that no matter where you learned cooking and entertaining—at your mother's knee, at school, or by working it out for yourself—you eventually come to see that a party requires preparation and planning. Trust me. All parties, whether large or small, for six-year-olds or thirty-somethings, for drinks or dinner, go so much more smoothly when things are thought through and laid out carefully.

nice to have your efforts appreciated, especially by a friend. But I had to smile. It was as if she thought I waved a magic wand or pulled a bunny out of a top hat. It was then I realized she didn't know my secret: the key to successful entertaining is planning.

Planning makes everything easier, and saves time too. When it seems like there is so much to do—and so little time—it can be easy to lose track of what you're trying to achieve and waste precious time on unnecessary shopping trips, searching for mislaid flatware, or dealing with the discovery that a last minute project isn't as easy as you had expected. Planning thoroughly allows you to see through the many layers of an event and break the party down into manageable categories. If you consider all the elements of the party ahead, use checklists, and work out timelines, you can create a framework that will prepare you for anything you might encounter when entertaining. That's a promise.

If planning is the paperwork part of entertaining—all about sitting down, thinking things through, and laying out on paper what you need to do when—then organizing is the active part. It's following through on the plans, timelines, and checklists that you draw up. It's sorting out your entertaining supplies, your music collection, and your kitchen cupboards so that they are arranged efficiently. Planning and organizing go hand in hand. Each makes it

By keeping your supplies organized and at hand, by laying out what you're trying to achieve and how to get there, you will give yourself the time to enjoy the pleasures that entertaining can bring. Being organized will allow you to put your creative touch on everything you do.

as it does to plan. ELEANOR ROOSEVELT

easier to do the other, and together they ease the workload of entertaining, enabling you to enjoy both the process and the party.

YOUR PARTY PLANNING JOURNAL

The first thing I do when planning a party is to get out my party planning journal. It's where I jot down my ideas and keep all the details about my event together—everything from the guest list, to the style of table setting, to the food I'll be serving, and the music I'll be playing. I wish I could claim to have invented the concept of the party planning journal, but it's an evolution of the style file, born out of the frustration of sifting through notes that I had kept on scraps of paper. Think of this as a living example of that old saying, "A place for everything and everything in its place."

project PARTY PLANNING JOURNAL

A party planning journal is basically a notebook with dividers and pockets. I use an 8½ x 11-inch notebook because I don't want to have too many details crammed together on a page. I want to be able to see and find things easily—and I want it to look good. If I see a beautiful notebook that is large enough and has dividers, then I'll buy it. Otherwise I might buy a plain notebook and cover it with fabric and add pockets, whatever it needs to become functional. The journal is a great way to keep the whole event organized, from planning the party through the execution of the event. I put every piece of information about my party in this journal so I know where to find things. Doing this definitely saves time. I'll keep a copy of the guest list and who has RSVP'd, and if the recipes for my party come from several different cookbooks, I'll photocopy them and place them in the pockets. This helps not only for menu planning, but for grocery shopping and cooking as well.

For every party you throw make a section in your journal for each of the seven basic elements of entertaining:

1. Type of party
2. Invitation
3. Menu
4. Drinks
5. Table
6. Atmosphere
7. Favors/Extras

Your journal will help keep track of your thoughts and ideas, and it will also become an invaluable reference tool when planning future events. After your party, you can record what worked and what didn't, adding notes and ideas for next time.

WHAT'S IN YOUR ENTERTAINING ARSENAL?

I often find that much of what I create, whether it's a new way of setting the table or a crafty project, depends on what I have at hand. So organizing my supplies for entertaining really makes a difference. As my mom once told me when I phoned her in frustration at not being able to find some soup bowls that I'd planned a meal around, "It doesn't matter what you have if you can't find it." Since that annoying day, I've organized my supplies into what I call arsenals. I have one for crafting and one for entertaining. Basically a collection of things that make my tasks go quickly and easily, these arsenals are the repositories of all the inspirational and essential entertaining items and craft supplies I own—they're the tools of my trade.

My entertaining arsenal is a collection of serving pieces, tableware, and accessories. Having these items ready at hand helps me to have the types of parties I want to have.

Creating a complete arsenal is an investment and you might need to build up your collection over time.

Versatile pieces that can work well for both a Christmas buffet and a baby shower are the most efficient elements of an entertaining arsenal. When shopping for these foundation pieces think simple clean lines and neutral colors. Such quality dishes don't need to be expensive. If you have fine bone china that's great, be sure to use it but it's not necessary. Shop for plates in stores like Pottery Barn, Crate & Barrel, Target, or your favorite local haunt. Choose ones that look good and can mix and match with many different styles; be sure they have "weight" when you pick them up so that they feel good in your hand.

Later you can embellish your collection with more colorful, funky pieces, like pink scalloped salad plates that you wouldn't use all the time but can transform your whole table when paired with the basic pieces. My own arsenal is constantly growing as I add fun pieces for different looks. It's true, I'm a plateaholic and just can't resist collecting tableware—luckily I have plenty of closets.

ENTERTAINING ARSENAL

Use this checklist to help you get started with your own entertaining arsenal and to make note of what you just have to have now . . . and what can wait till later.

Serving supplies
- Plates (8)
- Bowls (8)
- Forks (8)
- Knives (8)
- Salad/dessert forks (8)
- Teaspoons (8)
- Soupspoons (8)
- Butter knife
- Wineglasses (8)
- Water glasses (8)
- Napkins (8)
- Serving tray
- Meat fork
- Large serving platter
- Coffee/tea cups and saucers (8)
- Cheese board
- Cheese knife

- Hors d'oeuvres plates (8)
- Candles and candle holders (2)
- Corkscrew
- Ice bucket/wine cooler

• Optional but nice to have
- Tablecloth
- Placemats (8)
- Napkin rings (8)
- Dessert plates or footed dessert bowls (8)
- Gravy boat
- Cake/pie server
- Salad set (serving fork and spoon)
- Large serving bowls
- Cake stand
- Bread baskets
- Pitcher
- Cocktail shaker

Linen Lore

As well as building a collection of plates and platters, you'll be adding napkins, tablecloths, and runners to your arsenal. Many people feel intimidated about how best to care for and store table linens. The main thing is to be sure to store them neatly pressed. Avoid pulling out wrinkled napkins and slaving over a hot iron just before the party. After an event, spot-treat linens and wash according to care instructions; some do not like drier treatment, many benefit from line drying. Some linens require dry cleaning, so watch out for that when you're making your purchases. (All that running to the cleaners can add to your entertaining costs.)

You don't have to press tablecloths or runners immediately after washing and drying; save the ironing for a quiet night when there's something good on TV. And don't forget to press your napkins at the same time. Once pressed, fold tablecloths lengthwise and drape over hangers. I use wooden hangers, but those wire hangers that dry cleaners use for slacks, the ones with cardboard tubes, work great too—not the all-wire ones; they'll make sharp creases. Hanging tablecloths is the best way to avoid creases and unnecessary touch-up pressing when it's time to set the table and there are many other things to do.

KEEP IT TOGETHER

It doesn't matter what

Create a home for your entertaining arsenal. Whether you keep your entertaining essentials in one small closet, have them in various spots in the kitchen, or throughout the house, they should be readily accessible. It's easy if you can keep everything together, but if that isn't possible think creatively and utilize what space you have. Maybe plates can go in one cupboard and large platters on the top shelf of the clothes closet. If you're not going to use your arsenal supplies every day, then keep them on those slightly out-of-reach top shelves of the kitchen cabinets and move the

stuff you use more frequently to lower shelves. The hall closet, an antique linen press if you're lucky enough to have one, two large cardboard boxes in the guest room, or a cheap and cheerful trunk from your favorite discount store—whatever works with the space you have, suits your style, and allows you to keep your entertaining arsenal where you'll be able to lay hands on it again is just right.

I have so much stuff for entertaining, a visitor to my house can find plates stored in drawers in just about any bureau or buffet. There are even plates in drawers in the

you have if you can't find it.

guest room! I keep it all together by having a list of what I have and where it is and if you can't store your entertaining arsenal in one place then a master list like this is a great idea. Create a list on your computer of just what's in your entertaining arsenal and where it is stored. Make a printout to keep on a bulletin board, in your party planning journal in a handy drawer, or even where you store most of your arsenal supplies—it's a great aide-mémoire. And don't be afraid to use what you have; the foundation pieces of your entertaining arsenal can be your everyday tableware—then you can store them in the kitchen and they'll always be

It might seem obvious, but I always have nuts: cashews, marcona almonds, or mixed spiced nuts in the pantry. They're the first thing I put into a pretty bowl when someone comes over. I do that, then lay out the other snacks. Crackers are another staple. I keep three different kinds because different crackers go best with different cheeses: buttery or whole wheat crackers; a plain wafer type; and a seasoned cracker, kind of like an everything bagel, which is good for mild, plainer

Stocking your pantry with easy-to-use party staples

close at hand. If you have silver flatware, definitely use it. Silver tarnishes if not used, so rather than have to clean it before an event, use it regularly.

BEYOND THE BASICS— THE ESSENTIAL FOOD AND DRINK PANTRY

Keeping some survival staples on hand will ensure that you're well stocked for last-minute get-togethers. These foods can also come in handy if the toast for that bruschetta burns, the tray of appetizers hits the deck, or a blown fuse temporarily shatters your prep schedule. Having my pantry stocked with these staples has saved me many times. They're so last-minute, but so good—kind of like an appetizer insurance policy.

cheeses. If you're pressed for time or space you can purchase a box of assorted crackers that will cover all these bases. Carr's makes a great selection and they're widely available. A vacuum-packed package of sliced sopresseta, prosciutto, or salami—one is all you need—will keep for months in the refrigerator. Then one round of cheese—something basic like Brie, or my favorite, Nevat, a soft goat cheese from Spain, or a semi-soft French cheese called Chaumes that is sold in grocery stores—is always in the fridge. Cheese for your party pantry should be unopened because it doesn't last long once exposed to air. (Not only that, you never want to serve food to your guests that looks like it's already been picked over.) Oh, and be sure to store a jar of mixed olives.

For those occasions when you want a little more, look in the gourmet store and supermarket for pre-prepared bases that can be used for appetizers. I adore an artichoke pesto that mixes with mayonnaise and bakes in the oven. It makes an irresistible hot dip when served with pita chips or buttery crackers. Other appetizer bases mix with cream cheese to make yummy spreads. And don't forget the freezer. Store-bought filo hors d'oeuvres, miniquiche, and little puff pastry bites usually need only about fifteen minutes in the oven and never fail to impress. If you're a bit more ambitious and enjoy cooking, devote an afternoon to stocking the freezer with homemade hors d'oeuvres. Freeze them on a baking tray then transfer to Tupperware containers. You can take out just as many as you need at one time.

All these cocktail party staples have a long shelf or refrigerator life; however, if you notice that the cheese or meat is getting close to its use-by date, then use it for snacks or dinner. Remember, whatever you choose to keep in your party pantry does not have to be overly elaborate or expensive. Just be sure to select items with quality ingredients that are easy to prepare and present to your guests.

is like having an appetizer insurance policy.

Life is really just a string of parties and I'm

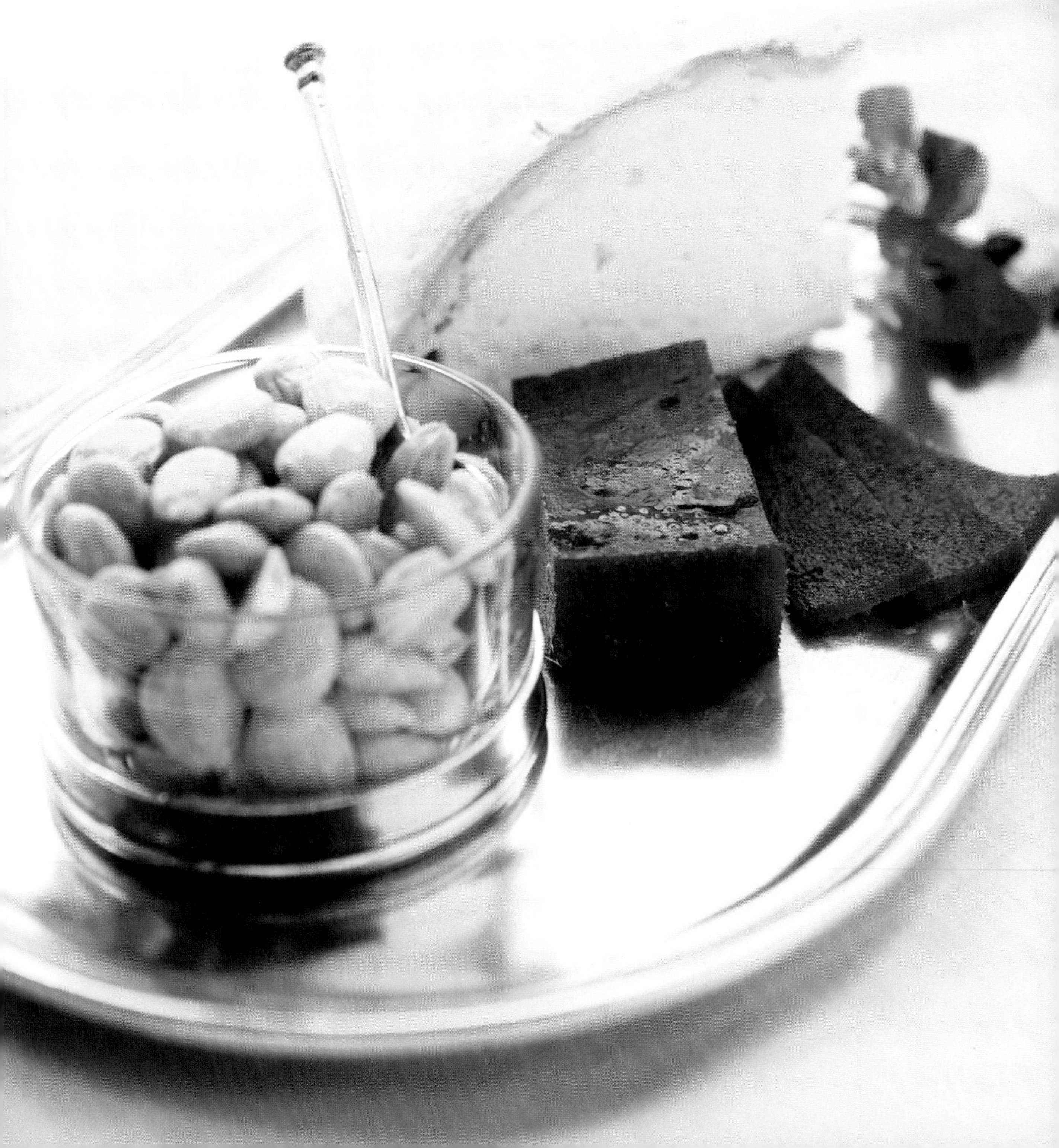

RAISING THE BAR: DRINKS

As for drinks, I keep a bottle of sparkling water in my refrigerator and am careful to replace it once opened. I also like to have a bottle of white wine in the fridge chilled and ready to go, but I have to watch or Todd will open it, and my preparations go astray. It might seem ritzy but I always keep a bottle of Champagne—or Prosecco which is cheaper but also really festive—in the refrigerator. I don't save it for special events; offering a guest a glass of Champagne makes any party seem that bit more special. A bottle of red wine rounds out my impromptu party drink prep. I'm not much of a beer drinker but if you are, then be sure to keep a six- or twelve-pack in the crisper drawer. If vodka is your thing, keep a bottle chilled and have favorite mixers on hand. Having drinks to offer at the start of an impromptu gathering is vital. If the party rocks on and drinks run low, someone can go to the store for more but everyone will still remember you as super-prepared.

IMPROMPTU PARTIES

Who was it who said, "A test of a good hostess is one who can entertain at a moment's notice"? The last-minute cocktail party is one of my favorite types of social gathering and it's being prepared that allows me to be spontaneous. When I meet a neighbor in the street or a friend stops by, I feel confident enough to invite them in because I know I have drinks and snacks to offer. Realize that they aren't coming to inspect your home; they're happy to be invited over. If you have ten minutes before someone arrives, do a quick pass with the vacuum, dim the lights, and light candles. If you bring your guests home with you, concentrate on making them feel comfortable. Get them a drink first and keep talking to them as you set out a bowl of nuts or other nibbles. Then reach for a platter for cheese and crackers. Never make them feel like you're running around frantically pulling things together. There's no magic to throwing a casual get-together like this. Keeping entertaining equipment organized and the pantry stocked makes it easy to pull off and enjoy a last-minute get-together.

The more you praise and celebrate your life, the more there is in life to celebrate. OPRAH WINFREY

CHAPTER 3

THINK *Like a* HOSTESS

Entertaining at home provides a wonderful opportunity to foster relationships with family and friends, and those acquaintances and colleagues whom you hope will become friends. Think about it: aren't the best times in life about enjoying yourself and the relationships you have? Too often it seems like life is filled with stress and busyness. You've got to go here and there. Got to do this or that. Entertaining can serve as a pleasant time-out from all the duties and obligations of daily life, an opportunity to carve out some time for real enjoyment. Entertaining is all about being hospitable, about treating others to a relaxing and comfortable experience, and having a great time yourself. Keep this thought in mind when you begin to plan a party and you will be well on your way to thinking like a hostess.

THE GRACIOUS HOSTESS

It might sound a little old-fashioned—"gracious" is not a word we hear that often today—but I think it's just the right adjective for a good hostess. Being gracious means being courteous, kind, tactful, and charming. I'd also add being diplomatic under fire and having a healthy dose of humor. Being a gracious hostess isn't about the food you serve; more courses, more food, more fancy does not make you a good or gracious hostess. Nor is it about having a spotless house when company comes. It's about how you act in social situations and how you treat your guests, about making everyone feel comfortable in your home.

Being gracious is about making people feel welcome and comfortable in your own special way. Getting into the gracious hostess mindset not only makes things more relaxed for your guests, it helps you too. Your role is to be congenial and fun, not perfect; you're doing things in your own special way, reflecting your own personal style. It took me a while to work that out. When I first started entertaining there were a few occasions when I was a complete disaster. I tried so hard to be perfect, but only succeeded in stressing myself out. At one party I was a total wreck by the time the first guest arrived because I

I love when you walk into a house and feel instantly

hadn't finished cleaning up or had time to change out of my scruffiest jeans. On another occasion I didn't come to the door at all because I was having a meltdown in the kitchen as my soufflé (yes soufflé!) was less than perfect. Trying to serve food that isn't comfortable to you or is beyond your culinary skills does not make for a fun event, nor does trying to craft a party you're not ready for. If you're not comfortable making decorations, buy some and concentrate on having excellent party music, if that's more a reflection of who you are. Remember: it's about pleasure, not perfection.

welcome – like you're in the heart of something. MINNIE DRIVER

BE MY GUEST

First and foremost, being a gracious hostess means considering who your guests are and bearing in mind that entertaining is never a one-size-fits-all proposition. You wouldn't wear a ball gown to a baseball game. And you wouldn't welcome a casual gathering of friends in the same way that you'd welcome your spouse's boss. Think first about your guests, about what they would like, and what they may need. If an elderly aunt is coming, for example, consider what you can do to make her feel at home. You might want to take her arm to help her up the stairs or give her a smaller portion at dinner so that she doesn't feel overwhelmed by what's in front of her. Likewise with children. You might set up a little table with paper and crayons so that they can amuse themselves somewhat quietly while

you and their parents—your friends—catch up on what's been happening since the last time you got together.

Sometimes a guest may have specific needs. If your brother's fiancée has extreme pet allergies, then don your gracious hostess hat and send your beloved dog to your neighbors for the duration of the party. If a dinner party guest alerts you to a newly discovered shellfish allergy ahead of time, accommodate that dietary restriction when you plan the menu. It's much easier to be gracious when guests inform you of special needs in advance of the party, but even if they turn to you as you pass the dinner plates and say, "I've just become vegetarian," keep that gracious hat on. No one expects you to whip up a different entrée, just offer the new vegetarian any parts of the meal that suit her diet.

Perhaps the true test of a gracious hostess is how well she handles things when they don't go as planned. Despite the best of preparations and organizing, in entertaining, much like in life, things can go wrong—and will. The hostess' mantra is "When things don't go perfectly, roll with the punch." And the best way to be prepared for things that do go wrong is to prepare your attitude before the party and remember that you're entertaining because you want to spend time with the people you care about and create memories with them. At the end of the day, the food or the table or the outfit you wore really doesn't matter. If you remain calm, you can't go wrong. And, when all else fails, try to find the humor in the situation and your guests will inevitably find it too. Honestly, learning to laugh at myself when things go awry is one of the best lessons I have ever learned. (I only wish I'd realized that before I tried to make that dratted soufflé.)

Your role is to be gracious and fun, not perfect.

A QUESTION OF ETIQUETTE

Q: Should the hostess answer her phone if it rings during dinner?
A: No, not unless it could be a late guest calling. When everyone has sat down to eat it's best to keep your focus on the guests at the table. It's for occasions like this that voice mail was invented.

Q: What do you do if a guest arrives late for dinner—and the rest of the party is just about to start dessert?
A: If they didn't even call to tell you they got stuck in traffic or at the office or whatever it was—well, that's just plain bad manners. Even so, act graciously. Bring them to the table, introduce them to the other guests, then ask if they'd like to join you all for dessert, or if they'd rather have some dinner first.

Q: Or worse—what do you do if a guest arrives *early?*
A: If someone arrives early, so early that you haven't changed yet, hopefully they'll be polite enough to offer to lend a hand. In this situation accept the offer graciously. Perhaps they can light the candles and put on the music, arrange the hors d'oeuvres on a platter, or even make a last-minute run to the store for additional ice. If the guest arrives just fifteen minutes ahead of time (unfashionably early instead of fashionably late), invite them into the kitchen to have a glass of wine as you do your last-minute prep—or buy yourself a few minutes by sending them out into the garden to admire your new roses.

A STITCH IN TIME—PRACTICAL TIPS FOR THE GOOD HOSTESS

Anytime you invite guests to your home there's a chance things may get spilled, broken, or otherwise damaged. As a good hostess, you should never show displeasure or anger should such things happen. Think about how mortified you felt when you broke a glass at your friend's house or spilled curried chicken on someone else's white linen cloth. What about the time you spilled red wine on the upholstered chair and your less-than-gracious hostess proclaimed to every-body the cost of the fabric! Your guest will already be embarrassed, so your job as hostess is to reassure them that everything is OK and fixable. You can cry about it later once the guests go home. When a *whoops* event happens, smile, reassure the shaken guest that you aren't mad, and fix the damage as best you can without disrupting the flow of the party. Here are some tips to deal with accidents that often occur when you have company.

RX FOR STAINS

Immediate action is your best defense against stains. Blot, don't scrub. And apply the remedy to the stained area only, testing first on a hidden area to make sure that the remedy is appropriate for this particular fabric.

Red Wine: Blot stain with a colorfast towel, then saturate with white wine. Blot with a clean towel and apply club soda. Leave laundering or cleaning with a carpet cleaner until after your guests have left.

White Wine: White wine is easier to deal with than red. Just flush with cool water, then apply an enzyme detergent (check the product label) and launder as usual.

Grease Stains: Fresh grease stains such as oil, butter, mayonnaise, or vinaigrette can be sprinkled with cornstarch or talcum powder to absorb the grease. Then treat the stain with a stain remover such as Shout or Spray 'n Wash, or a mixture of baking soda and dish detergent.

Fruit and Vegetable Stains: Stains such as juice and jam

are best treated with a commercial stain remover such as Shout or Spray 'n Wash to remove the sugars. If this doesn't remove all the color, then once your guests have gone home, flush the stain with white vinegar followed by hydro-gen peroxide. Apply an enzyme detergent to remove any residue before laundering.

Anything that is not washable is best treated by the dry cleaner.

WAXIDENT — CANDLE WAX SPILLS

Candle wax can be tricky to remove; it all depends on what material it was spilled on.

- If candle wax spills on your wooden table, soften it with a hairdryer, then using a vinegar and water solution along with a sponge, wipe the melted wax away. Never use a knife to try and scrape wax from your table—unless you want a scratched table.
- If hot wax has found its way onto your table linens, rub the wax with an ice cube, then take a butter knife and scrape or lift off as much wax as possible from the fabric. Once you have removed the larger pieces, place the waxed area of the tablecloth on an ironing board. Put a paper grocery bag or paper towels below and on top of the stain, then run a warm iron over the area to transfer the wax residue onto the paper or paper towel. Reposition the paper so a fresh spot is over the wax and continue ironing to absorb all of the wax. Repeat until all wax is removed. Use this same technique to remove wax from carpets or rugs.

PARTY CRASHERS — SOMETHING GETS BROKEN

Maybe it was just a wineglass or maybe it was an heir-loom plate. Whatever is broken your reaction should be the same. Don't ever let your guest know you're devas-tated. Speed to the accident scene with a replacement glass or plate, quickly and cheerfully pick up the broken pieces. Then change the focus from the accident back to the party fun. If the broken item has sentimental value, try to save all the pieces, no matter how small. Porcelain repair or china restoration specialists can work magic with broken porcelain.

PLAN B

One of my mottos really is "Be prepared." It underpins all my party planning. Chances are, as long as you have tried out all the recipes before your party, all the food will turn out just fine. Still, it definitely pays to be prepared with Plan B, because even an experienced cook such as my heroine Julia Child has burned and dropped dinners. And some-times even professionals find that a recipe fails.

If your special appetizer bombs, just pull out the cheese and crackers that form part of your party pantry. If the flourless chocolate cake is not only flourless, but black as charcoal, then

reach for the insurance-policy ice cream and hot fudge sauce. If your main course is burned, butchered, or otherwise broken, try to keep things in perspective and know that there is always a solution, even if it's a large cardboard box marked "pizza."

Remember: no matter what goes wrong, your best response is a smile.

TOASTS AND HOW TO MAKE THEM

The Art of the Toast

Not every party requires a toast; a perfectly fabulous evening can be had without everyone toasting each other but when you're hosting a party with a guest of honor, a toast is a suitably reverential thing. As the hostess you should always be the first person to toast the guest of honor and you should stand when making a toast. A gentle tap on a wine or water glass is the time-honored way of getting everyone's attention. Be prepared—know what you want to say ahead of time, be brief and stay simple, then wait for the applause. Here are some of my favorites:

May the best of happiness, honor, and fortune keep with you.

Here's to a full belly, a heavy purse, and a light heart.

May our house always be too small to hold all our friends.

Here's to a friend. He knows you well and likes you just the same.

Here's to cold nights, warm friends, and a good drink to give them.

Make the most of life while you may, Life is short and wears away!
(William Oldys)

May the most you wish for be the least you get.

Over time I've realized that being a gracious hostess is not just one of the three basic tenets of entertaining, it's *the* single most important element. Nothing makes your guests feel more uncomfortable than a blatant reminder of how hard you have worked preparing dinner—for them! From the second your guests arrive, the focus should be on your company and making them feel welcome and comfortable, not on perfecting details or rearranging things.

CHAPTER 4

Imagine

THAT

Once you're comfortable with your style, have acknowledged the importance of being prepared and organized, and have settled into the gracious hostess mindset, it's time to put your newfound savvy to work imagining and planning your party. It's time to have some fun.

First off you need to work out what kind of party you'd like to have and the overall effect you're hoping to achieve. Then you'll need to make a detailed party timetable. That might not sound like a lot of fun, but careful planning really will make everything much more manageable. Certainly it will help to cut down on those nasty surprises, like forgetting to pick up ice or polish the silverware. So no matter how far ahead of time you decide to throw a party (or how close to the day!), sit down and draw up a schedule. Think of it as your game plan.

It's important to marry the joy of inspiration with the hard realities of time and money . . . remember there is no perfect party, just the party that's perfect for you.

Ideally you'll start your game plan a month ahead, but if you don't have that much time, work with what you have. Just know that the less time you have to prepare, the less complicated your party should be. That sounds so obvious you probably can't believe it's here in print, but it's easy to get carried away with ideas and inspiration, and it's easy to forget that it's important to marry the joy of inspiration with the hard realities of time and money. As you start on the road to party nirvana, remember there is no perfect party, just the party that's perfect for you.

INSPIRATION BOARD

An inspiration board can be a great tool to get you in the mood for the party to come. Think of it as a surrogate style file where you can pin all the elements that inspire ideas for your party. Anything goes. My inspiration board is a corkboard that hangs on the wall in my craft room. Hang yours wherever you'll see it frequently—in the study, the kitchen,

in the bedroom. If you don't want to hang it just lean it against the wall somewhere where it's obvious, on the hall table or a kitchen counter maybe.

You might not know much about the party you're going to have when you start your inspiration board. It might be just that you know you're having six guests for dinner. But as you flip through magazines and the colors of a room jump out at you, tear out that page and pin it up. A swatch of fabric, a picture of a bird, a cool looking cocktail in a distinctive glass—whatever calls out to you, pin it up. It may inspire the look of your table or the drinks you serve. You may end up taking it off the board when you decide later that it doesn't fit with what you're doing, and that's okay. In the beginning it's all about process and inspiration, so if you have an eclectic mix of weird stuff that reminds you of what you're working toward, great. There's something about putting everything together in one spot that keeps your mind focused on the task at hand yet leaves room for creativity. Enjoy it.

THE SEVEN ELEMENTS OF PARTY PLANNING

Think of the following points as the big seven, the elements that you need to think about in order to crystallize the ideas for your party. We'll be looking at numbers two to seven in more detail in the following chapters. For now we'll start at the beginning, with number one.

1. WHAT TYPE OF PARTY?

First off you need to decide what type of party you want to have. This might be decided by why you're having a party in the first place. Your best friend is getting married and you're going to host her shower. It's your first Christmas in your new home and you want to invite the neighbors over. Often, though, there isn't a birthday or big event to commemorate, just the desire to host a party or a feeling that you need to return the hospitality of friends who've entertained you so many times. You might think there are just two kinds of parties, dinner parties (fewer people) and large gatherings; actually I divide party possibilities into four main categories:

DAYTIME PARTIES: LUNCHEONS, BRUNCHES, OR TEAS Most events can be held in the daytime; a cocktail party is the obvious exception—best left till the sun is going down. Daytime parties are versatile and can be sit-down lunches, brunches, or buffets.

COCKTAIL PARTY When you invite a group over for drinks or a wine tasting you'll serve snacks, tapas, or hors d'oeuvres and not a full meal, so it's a great way to entertain a larger group. As the atmosphere is less formal than at a sit-down event, the cocktail party is a good way to introduce people such as old friends from college and new work friends. They all get chatting over a drink or two. And everyone loves this kind of casual, mingling party with great wine and a lot of cheese.

BUFFET The best way to feed a larger crowd, buffets are wonderful for holiday entertaining and family parties or get-togethers. They're extremely versatile. You can serve a four-course buffet, clearing the buffet between courses, or place all the food on the buffet so guests can take what they want when they like. Another delicious option is a dessert-only buffet.

SIT-DOWN DINNER A sit-down dinner is a more intimate venue than a larger party and gives everyone a chance to talk to each other and admire your centerpiece. It can be a casual supper in the kitchen or a formal, multicourse meal in the dining room. Don't despair if you don't have a "proper" dining room. The invitation, menu, look of the table, and general atmosphere of the occasion are what mark it as formal, not where your table is located or how large it is.

PRACTICAL MAKES PERFECT

Now that you know what's possible you'll need to think about what's practical. Think about the space you have and where you'll set the stage for your event. I'm assuming you're throwing a party at your home, but still you'll need to decide on the location within your home. The type of party you're having usually determines which room or rooms you'll have it in: a larger party will likely be in your family room or great room, whereas a sit-down dinner may begin with drinks in one room, moving to the dining room for the meal itself. Also consider the workload. Much as I love to entertain, I host only sit-down dinners for eight or less. If I want to invite more people I'll make it a buffet or a drinks party. This isn't so much a consideration of the size of my table as it is a recognition of the amount of work involved. I find it's easy to plate and serve a meal for six; eight is a little harder but I can do it. But I know my limitations, and eight is it. The exception to that rule is if I have a cohost; if Todd is going to help me in the kitchen; or best of all, if a close girlfriend and I throw the party together (Let's do it again sometime soon Dawn!), then I'll invite more folks to a sit-down. Obviously if you're having help, like caterers to do the cooking or waiters to serve and clean up, then these rules don't apply. If it's just little-old-you or me in the kitchen then I suggest sticking to eight or less around the dinner table.

DOLLARS AND SENSE The next question is a big one: how much? A sit-down dinner could cost as little as $7 per person or could easily go over $35 per person. A casual meal, say Mexican food with beer, would keep costs down. Serving different wines with each course or expensive cuts of beef or wild salmon will push up the price. If you're watching the dollars, consider hosting a daytime party as generally less or no alcohol is served during the day, and often the food served is a little lighter too. You also don't need candles during the day either. Be realistic in your planning and consider the costs of things. You might want to serve beluga caviar to twenty guests at your cocktail party, but if it interferes with being able to pay the electric bill, maybe it's not such a good idea. (Still, if you're stuck on the notion of caviar, try American sturgeon caviar. It's less than half the price of its Russian counterpart and still has that Wow! factor.) Entertaining is not free but you're doing it to share a special experience with your friends, so make a special party that works for your budget.

IT'S ABOUT TIME I'll let you in on a secret: any type of party can be scaled to the time you have available. If you have a lot of time and energy to spare you can create favors and decorations and make all the food from scratch. If time is more limited you might want to keep décor to a minimum or use some premade food in your menu. A cocktail party may be easier to pull off and less expensive than a sit-down dinner, but not always. Guests are "grazing"not dining, so it will keep costs down. Be careful. It might sound like an easy option—and it can be—but it all depends on what food you choose to serve and whether you make everything from scratch or incorporate some premade or partially premade dishes, which can nudge the price up. A casual sit-down dinner is generally less work than a formal sit-down dinner and can take less time to prepare. I often serve the salad and main course together for a casual supper, then it's just a matter of clearing those dishes and bringing out dessert. A more formal dinner requires more courses and more plates and flatware.

There are no easy rules when it comes to judging party prep and planning time. Just be guided by common sense and the knowledge that the more elaborate the party, the more time you'll need.

YOUR PARTY PLANNING JOURNAL

Once you've given due consideration to this big first question—What Type of Party—it's time to get out your party planning journal, sit in a comfy chair and jot down your ideas. Then brainstorm about the rest of the big seven and use your party planning journal for all your ideas, notes, and lists. By keeping everything about the party together in one place you'll solve the problem of trying to find that scrap of paper with the great idea. You won't have to search for it because it'll be in your journal. . . . Won't it?!

2. INVITATIONS

Now that you know what type of party and roughly how many people, you're ready to think about invitations. What type of invitation suits the party you're planning? Do you want to make invitations or buy them? Let your imagination go wild and think about what might work as an invitation.

3. MENU

It's not time to get your cookbooks out yet; what you need to think about now is what type of food will you serve. What will work for your particular type of party, your budget, and your culinary skills? Brainstorm how many courses are feasible and if you fancy making an all-Indian menu or a really seasonal feast, if you want to serve chicken as a main course or use mostly store-bought food for your hors d'oeuvres. Put all your thoughts down in your journal.

4. DRINKS

Explore your options. There are many! If you have definite ideas on a cocktail or other drink that seems just right, note them in your journal.

5. TABLE

If you've already pinned some pictures or swatches on your inspiration board you might have colors already in mind for the table at your party. Maybe you know that you want red accents for your entertaining-arsenal cream-colored dinner plates. Think creatively here and you can't go wrong.

6. ATMOSPHERE

Atmosphere is everything taken together, the whole that's larger the sum of all its parts. There are many things you can do to create the right atmosphere for your event, whether it's as obvious as making themed decorations for a birthday party or as subtle as lighting candles to create a mood. Music also contributes to the mood. Considered which group of music CDs will enhance your party atmosphere.

7. FAVORS

Do you want to make or buy party favors to give? Do you have time or money for favors? If something has to hit the chopping block, you can't cut food and drinks, but you can dispense with the favors. In a way, that's what makes them so special—people don't expect them, but love getting them.

TIMELINE

The secret to hosting a successful party is all about managing your time and staggering preparation. Rather than going crazy for the three days immediately preceding the party, make a detailed timetable of what you need to do before the event, then plot out when you can do it. The timeline here is specific to hosting a dinner party; nevertheless, many elements remain the same for a buffet or cocktail party. This should give you an idea of what can be done—and when. Use it as a general outline for your own party.

ONE MONTH OUT

- Plan your menu and drinks.
- Create your shopping lists: Grocery store lists for non-perishables, bar supplies, perishables, and last-minute items like ice.
- Wine or liquor store list.
- Craft and art store supplies for projects and other decorations.
- Inspect your plates, glasses, flatware, and serving pieces—plan the look of your table, set a sample place setting to check if your idea works, and see if you need any additional items and purchase them.
- Make (or buy) and send invitations.

TWO WEEKS PRIOR

- Shop for nonperishable food including dried and frozen ingredients.
- Buy wine and any other alcoholic beverages.
- Cook anything that can be made ahead and frozen in a ovenproof container, ready to be reheated on the day.
- Make favors.

ONE WEEK BEFORE

- Wash any serving pieces, glasses, utensils, pitchers, or plates that you have not used in a while.
- Assemble music or create a CD.
- Check or set up CD player or iPod.
- Plan where drinks will be served and where hors d'oeuvres will be set out.

THREE DAYS PRIOR

- Prepare any part of the meal you can make in advance—this includes any preliminary steps such as chopping or prep work that can save you time when cooking the meal.
- Clean the bathrooms and set out clean towels, new soap, and extra rolls of toilet paper.
- Set up the bar or drinks table.

THE DAY BEFORE

- Buy perishable foods.
- Prepare food that can be refrigerated.
- Remove any dishes from the freezer to thaw in the refrigerator.
- Buy flowers and arrange them; if not using flowers, assemble the centerpiece.
- Decorate if using themed decorations.
- Set the dinner table; set out wine glasses and hors d'oeuvres serving pieces.

THE MORNING OF THE PARTY

- Shop for last-minute supplies such as ice and fresh bread.

- Chop and prepare salad ingredients and cover with a damp paper towel in the fridge.

THE AFTERNOON OF THE PARTY

- Prepare the remaining salad ingredients and add to salad bowl.
- Make the dessert and bake if required.
- Make any hors d'oeuvres (if not made ahead and frozen, or store-bought).
- Spot-clean the kitchen.
- Do last-minute bathroom check.

TWO HOURS BEFORE

- Finish final dessert preparations.
- Place cheese and crackers on a platter (if using bread, do not set out until later).
- Fill coffeepot with water and set up the filter and coffee.
- Preheat the oven.

ONE HOUR BEFORE

- Bake or reheat hors d'oeuvres.
- Open the wine, recork it, and chill white wine in an ice bucket.
- Begin cooking or reheating main course.

15 MINUTES BEFORE GUESTS ARRIVE

- Arrange hors d'oeuvres on platters; light candles; start music.

WHEN THE GUESTS ARRIVE

- Greet guests at door, take coats, and offer them a glass of wine.
- If needed, remove main course from oven and let rest 20 minutes.

15 MINUTES BEFORE DINNER

- Remove the salad from refrigerator.
- Heat and slice the bread, place bread in basket on table.
- Fill water glasses.
- Add dressing to salad and toss.

Smart Shopping

Do as much shopping in advance as possible; you can fit a lot more into the last few hours before the party if you don't have to dash off to the store. Similarly, when you make a shopping list always check it at least twice to make sure you haven't forgotten anything. If you can cut down on last-minute panic runs for essential ingredients (or because you discover at the eleventh hour that you're low on toilet paper), you'll be less stressed and have a much better time. Many people focus on their menu when compiling shopping lists but don't remember all the other things they'll need, nonfood and beverage items like garbage bags, ice, and candles.

DINNERTIME

• Place salad on the dinner table.

• Start the coffee brewing.

DURING DINNER

• Remove salad and place main course on dinner table.

• Refill water and wine glasses and offer second helpings.

AFTER THE MAIN COURSE

• Remove plates; serve dessert; offer coffee or tea.

AFTER DESSERT

• Suggest that everyone retire to more comfortable surroundings such as the family room.

As you plan your party, you might find if helpful to make a master shopping list, then break it down into lists per trip or per store. For example, you should count on making at least three trips to the grocery store: one trip for non-perishables and bar supplies; a second trip for perishables a couple of days before the party; and a final trip on the day of the party for last minute items like ice and bread.

A trip to the craft store for craft supplies and a visit to the wine or liquor store to stock up on drinks is also in your immediate future.

IT'S MY PARTY

I'll be right there with you as I guide you through planning and hosting your party. In fact, you can follow my progress as I plan and pull off my own event, a formal sit-down dinner for eight for my husband Todd's birthday. It's going to be a special dress-up occasion for three of Todd's close friends and their partners, as well as Todd and me of course. They've all been to our house before, but this time I'm planning something above and beyond what I normally do. Actually, it's the kind of party you wear a little black dress to, so I'm going to call it my Little Black Dress Dinner Party.

I've marked my party for a Saturday one month away. That's the first notation in my party planning journal. The dinner has to be on a Saturday because most of our friends have worked hard all day and are just too plain tired to get dressed up and go out on a Friday. Besides, there's so much Friday traffic to fight in Atlanta, and with a sit-down meal I want to be sure that everyone gets here on time, so Saturday it is. I'll invite my guests for 7:30 P.M., and plan on serving dinner at 8:00 or 8:15. I'm not making a birthday cake for the party because it's not his actual birthday. He can have cake and candles on his actual birthday, but for this dinner we'll have a grown-up dessert—but it has to be even better tasting than cake . . . what could that be? I'll think about that later, now I need to think about invitations.

The best thing about a cocktail party
is being asked to it.

GERALD NACHMAN

PALACES OF SICILY

Mr. and Mrs. Todd Kennedy
3527 West Pacas Ferry Road
Atlanta, Georgia 30339

CHAPTER 5

You're INVITED

I love finding a heavy envelope among the flurry of bills and supermarket circulars in my mailbox. An unusually sized or brightly colored envelope in the midst of all that manila and newsprint can really make my day. In fact, receiving an invitation today is just as exciting for me as it was when I was a little girl and a party invitation would give me butterflies as I anticipated all the games, fun, and cake to come.

Call me old-fashioned, but I really do think it's a shame that so many people don't bother with invitations anymore. You might think they seem a bit formal, only necessary for weddings or showers. Or maybe a little juvenile—the six-year-old birthday scenario. But I believe they're important for the way in which they convey the tone and thought behind a party. An invitation doesn't have to have bells and whistles (though I have to admit that I do love bells and whistles), and it doesn't have to be constructed out of posh, expensive paper, but it should grab your guests' attention and get them excited about the good times ahead.

I guess you could say I'm a stickler about invitations. Certainly it's one of those times when I'm a true traditional-ist, when I channel Emily Post and the niceties of proper etiquette. The only time I invite people by phone is for a casual meal, a "hey-can-you-come-over-for-a-cookout-this-Saturday?" kind of impromptu event. But I never email my invitations. I know that a lot of people like email invites, especially for last-minute parties. And even though they're a handy way to stretch a budget, they're just not my thing. Don't get me wrong, I love my computer, but I like to use it to make my own invitations so that I can express my style and the style of the party too. That's not to say that email invitations are improper, just that they're not me. If you do like to email invitations, be sure to pay particular attention to the wording you use so that you can still convey the personality of the party. Me, I'll stick to snail mail.

An imaginative invitation can heighten the expectations surrounding your party and often means a better turnout. When it seems that everyone is so overscheduled with work and more work, family responsibilities, dental appointments, and engine tune-ups, how nice it is for your friends to receive something positive, an envelope they can tear open gleefully, a date to circle on the calendar.

BE MY GUEST

Before you decide on the type of invitation you want to send, start jotting down who you are required to invite and mull over who else it would be good to ask. I have this belief that all guest lists start life on the back of an envelope while you're in line at the bank. Try not to get bogged down with various names scribbled on too many different bits of paper. Move to a notepad or your party planning journal so that once you've come up with the guest list you can add mailing addresses or just type it all into the computer.

When considering whom to invite, think about the personalities of potential guests and if they would make an interesting mix. It might be a group who already know each other; old friends from college who don't get to see each other that often, your neighbors, a mix of family and close friends. Or opt for a lively combination of folks who don't already know each other but should. Remember, you do not have to have all couples or all singles at a party or even people of the same age. Aim for a good balance. Keep in mind that the right mix of people really makes the party, so invite guests who are likely to be interested in one another and have things to talk about.

Be clear on whom you're inviting. If you'd like a couple to attend, put both their names on the front of the envelope; if you're only inviting one of them, put only one name on the

envelope; and if you're happy for someone to bring a partner or friend, write "and guest" on the envelope so he or she knows it's all right to bring a companion.

Once you've figured out whom you are going to invite, make a final guest list to keep by the phone and use it to keep track of who is coming when people RSVP.

RÉPONDEZ, S'IL VOUS PLAÎT

You've got to hand it to the French. RSVP seems much more inviting than its English counterpart: "Reply if you please" just doesn't have the same allure. I figure that everyone understands this classic French phrase, so I always use it on my invitations. I also put my name and phone number at the bottom of the party details to make it easy for the invitees to respond to my fabulous invitation. Even when you make it clear and give them all the details, not everyone remembers to RSVP. If it's getting close to the date of your event, say, three days before and you're ready to do your final food shopping, call the guests who still have not responded. You need to know if they will be joining you so you can make a final head count for food and drinks and avoid wasting your funds on supplies for guests who don't show.

Turn Left at the Traffic Light

I remember the time that Todd and I got lost on the way to a dinner party. Our friends had recently moved and we weren't familiar with their new neighborhood. We took a wrong turn somewhere and couldn't seem to find their house. Worst of all, there was absolutely no one around to ask for directions. After six circuits of the same blocks we called—thank heavens for cell phones—and of course found out we were only one street away. We'd been a tad late leaving home that night and what with getting lost, they had started dinner without us. We felt awful. Luckily our hosts were gracious and soon made us feel better. Still, I learned the importance of driving directions or a map if your company is not familiar with your address.

SAVE THE DATE

How far ahead should invites be sent? It depends on the type of party and the time of year. During the holidays people's calendars fill up quickly so you may want to allow a little more time than suggested here.

For a tea or luncheon: 2 weeks

For a baby or wedding shower: 3 weeks

For a cocktail party: 2–4 weeks

For an informal dinner: 3 weeks

For a formal dinner: 3–6 weeks

GREAT EXPECTATIONS

Your invitation should reflect the personality of your party: formal or casual, kitschy, fun, or totally traditional like a Thanksgiving feast. That's not to say you have to send a beach towel as the invitation for a pool party (although that's a provocative idea); the colors, paper, and fonts you choose can suggest the mood of the event. The invitation should also include information on the type of event, who's hosting it, the location, and at what date and time. You should also include other information that is specific to the party. If you're throwing a pool party, for example, remind your guests to bring their own towels. If certain dress is required for a theme party, or if you're requesting that no presents be given at the birthday bash you're throwing, mention that too.

So—consider the form and style of invitation you'd like to send and how you want it to reflect the type of event you are hosting. Maybe you'd like a simple card-stock invitation. Maybe you want something fun and whimsical. Or maybe classic and elegant best suits you and your party? Consider the theme and formality of the party and think about how much time you have to devote to creating invitations. Also, how many guests will you be inviting? An

Dinner and Dancing
immediately following the ceremony
Debussy Ballroom
Château Elan

Black Tie

Mr. and Mrs. Christopher Todd Kennedy

PLEASE JOIN US FOR

COCKTAILS, DINNER AND DANCING

AT FIVE O'CLOCK IN THE EVENING

DRUID HILLS GOLF CLUB

740 CLIFTON ROAD NE

ATLANTA, GEORGIA

Doctor and Mrs. Paul Vincent Hartman
request the honour of your presence
at the marriage of their daughter
Kimberly Suzanne
to
Mr. Christopher Todd Kennedy
Saturday, the sixth of June
One thousand nine hundred and ninety~eight
at seven o'clock in the evening
First Presbyterian Church
Athens, Georgia

K

KIMBERLY KENNEDY

3527 West Paces Ferry Road
Atlanta, Georgia 30339
404 555 1234

kimberly@kimberlykennedy.com

Reception

immediately following the ceremony

Athens Country Club

Please join us for a

Casual Supper

Saturday, March 19th

6:30 pm

Todd and Kimberly Kennedy

3527 West Paces Ferry Road

Atlanta, Georgia

R.S.V.P.

404-555-1234

elaborate invitation is fun to make maybe four times, so it is perfect for an intimate dinner party. But do you really want to reproduce a labor-intensive project for twenty guests? (And while we're talking about practical matters, don't forget to include the cost of the invitations in your party budget—that means envelopes and postage too.)

I delight in sending quirky invitations, but there are times when they are just not suitable. Simple white or ecru engraved invitations are best for momentous occasions such as weddings, births, and religious ceremonies. For these important times, a classic invitation is the best option. You will never regret it or feel that it is out of style. I save my creativity for the showers and parties that surround such events. Those are opportunities to really go wild with invitations. But before going wild I want to show you how to make a traditional invitation. It can be formal and elegant, suitable for grandparents and bosses, or pretty funky and fun, to suit your girlfriends' tastes—it all depends on the papers you choose and the fonts you use. It's a wonderfully versatile invitation and uses many of the same techniques I use in the other invitations I want to share with you.

project LAYERED CARD-STOCK INVITATION

This multilayered card-stock invitation is my basic invitation. When creating invitations on my computer I like to use at least two, preferably three different types of paper. For the base I always use card stock, a heavyweight paper, both for the function and the feel of the overall invite. The rigid nature of the card stock makes the invitation seem more important and of high quality.

I also like to use two other coordinating papers to create depth and texture. Depending on the overall look I am going for, sometimes I choose all three papers in the same color family and rely on different textures for interest. Other times I'll select contrasting colors. The only rule is that one of the coordinating papers *must* be printer friendly.

To get the layered effect, the card-stock base is cut the largest, the center portion is trimmed slightly smaller, and the top printed piece is cut the smallest and therefore "framed" by the other two papers. The end result looks much like a framed and matted picture.

When deciding on the size of your invitation keep in mind the envelope you plan to mail the invites in. I find it is best to cut the invite to the size of the envelope rather than try to find an envelope to fit a custom size.

Once the basic invitation is complete, I often embellish it with ribbon and different charms, buttons, or beads, because I like those little extras and think it makes the invitation even more unique. (And the envelope thicker!)

WHAT YOU'LL NEED

EQUIPMENT

- Computer and printer
- Paper cutter or scissors
- Ruler
- Hole punch (optional)

MATERIALS

For each invitation:
- 2 sheets coordinating paper, one sheet must be printer friendly
- 1 sheet card stock or heavyweight paper
- Spray mount adhesive or double stick tape
- Ribbon, $1/4$ to $1^{1}/2$ inches wide, can be wired or unwired (Optional)
- Embellishments such as buttons or charms (Optional)

WHAT YOU'LL DO

1. Select a fun font that goes with the theme or look of the party. Type the information, centering the text on the page.

2. Experiment with different font sizes. For example, for a dinner party in honor of a special friend, make the friend's name several point sizes larger than the rest of the information.

3. Once the invitation is typed, print a sample on a sheet of plain paper. Make any changes necessary then, once the wording is correct, print using the printer-friendly paper.

4. Use a paper cutter to cut card stock to 5 x 7 inches. Cut the coordinating paper so it is slightly smaller than the card stock, approximately $4^{1}/2$ x $6^{1}/2$ inches. Trim the printed page so it is slightly smaller than the coordinating paper, about $4^{5}/8$ x $6^{5}/8$ inches.

5. Use spray mount adhesive to attach the printed invitation to the paper, then attach the paper to the card stock.

Optional: The invitation can be embellished by punching two small holes $1/4$ inch apart in its top and running a ribbon through them. Other embellishments such as buttons or charms or beads can be attached to the ribbon.

The sky's the limit once you've mastered a classic invitation like the layered card-stock version shown here. You can play with size, shape, color, texture. Oh, and who says that an invitation has to be on paper? Not me for sure.

project DELIGHTFUL DIAPER INVITATION

This invitation always gets a great response. I made it for a friend's baby shower and everyone got so excited when they received the invite—I actually got calls from friends just to tell me how cute the invitation was. Some even brought the invitations to work to show their coworkers. Sending such a fun invite made my guests excited to see what I had planned for the shower itself. And the neat thing is, instead of throwing a plain paper invite out when the party was over, everyone kept their invitation. So now they have a memento from the shower.

Most important, even though it looks elaborate and adorable, this diaper invite is actually inexpensive to make—it costs less than getting invitations printed at a store. Each one costs only about $2.00 to make and mail.

Note: To ensure the best results, be sure to read the instructions on the iron-on paper package.

WHAT YOU'LL NEED

EQUIPMENT
- Computer and Printer
- Iron
- Scissors

MATERIALS
For each invitation:
- 1 sheet iron-on ink-jet printer paper
- 1 cloth diaper
- 2 diaper pins
- Ribbon or other embellishments such as charms and beads (optional)

WHAT YOU'LL DO

1. Open a new word processing document and type in the invitation details. Select font and format text. Once it is formatted to your liking, flip the text.* Print a sample on a plain piece of paper. If everything is correct, print on the iron-on paper and trim excess iron-on paper surrounding text.

2. Laying the diaper vertically, iron the invitation on the top of the diaper starting the text about three inches from the top.** Let cool and peel the back off the transfer.

3. To add more text, such as "It's a Girl," print text on iron-on paper (see above) and iron this piece of paper about 5 inches from the top of the *other* end of the diaper. Let cool and peel the back off the transfer. (See page 63, top left.) (The two pieces of text will be facing in opposite directions. Once the diaper is folded, they will both be right side up.)

4. Place diaper vertically, text side down. Fold sides in $2\frac{1}{2}$ inches. Fold bottom up 4 inches and top down $2\frac{1}{2}$ inches. Then fold left and right sides at an angle. (See page 63, top right.)

5. Fold bottom of diaper up so front is slightly lower than back. (See page 63, bottom left.)

6. Fold back top corners forward to meet front top corners and pin in place. (See page 63, bottom right.)

Optional: Ribbons or other embellishment can be attached to the ends of the pins.

---

*If you do not know how to flip text, check your word processing program's help file. Key search words include "mirror text," "flip," or "T-shirt transfer."

**Read the iron-on paper manufacturer's instructions before ironing the image onto fabric.

AN INVITATION WITH SUBSTANCE

For my Little Black Dress Dinner Party I wanted to create an invitation that would be different from the card-stock ones I often make, something that would reflect the special nature of the evening. I knew I wanted to incorporate texture—fabric, maybe?—and I knew I wanted it to have some substance so that the recipient would feel the weight in her hand when the invitation was taken out of the envelope. At the same time, I knew I wanted the party to have a rather fancy feel to it, sort of like a meal at a four-star restaurant.

Then I remembered those big prix fixe menus some restaurants have, the paper menus set in a cloth board or leather cover. That was my inspiration. I made a few sketches, got out the sewing machine, tried out my ideas and eventually got it to work—after a few false starts! I like that this invitation really sets the tone for a special event and hopefully it will get the others excited about coming, get them to dust off their party dresses and pull out a suit.

project SILK MENU INVITATION

I really love making this menu invitation. It's a three-fold design that acts as a traditional invitation, with all the important party information, as well as letting your guests know what the menu will be. It's a great way to get your guests excited about the dinner that is ahead. I like to display the menu on the larger center portion with the party details on one of the sides. You may use the remaining side to share wine selections for the evening or any other information you want to include such as directions to your home, information about the guest of honor, or a poem.

This menu invitation does take a bit more effort than the other invitations here but I think it's well worth making. It can be pretty much any size but the side wings will be half the width of the center section. I used one 8 x 10-inch piece of cardboard for my center so each side piece was 4 x 10 inches. When open, the overall invitation was 16 x 10 inches. I created a pattern from paper using these measurements and used the pattern to cut out two pieces of fabric per invitation. You don't have to use silk for this menu invitation; I chose it because it's so elegant but pretty much any fabric will work. And you can use any type of ribbon you like—wired or unwired, grosgrain, sheer, or silk.

WHAT YOU'LL NEED

EQUIPMENT

- Sewing machine
- Iron
- Glue gun and gluesticks
- Scissors

MATERIALS

For each invitation:

- Large sheet paper for pattern (can use a paper grocery store bag)
- 3 sheets printer-friendly paper
- 2 sheets coordinating card stock
- $\frac{1}{2}$ yard fabric
- Thread to match fabric
- 2 pieces 8 x 10-inch standard weight cardboard
- $\frac{1}{2}$ yard 1-inch ribbon
- 3 sheets coordinating paper
- Spray mount adhesive or double-stick tape

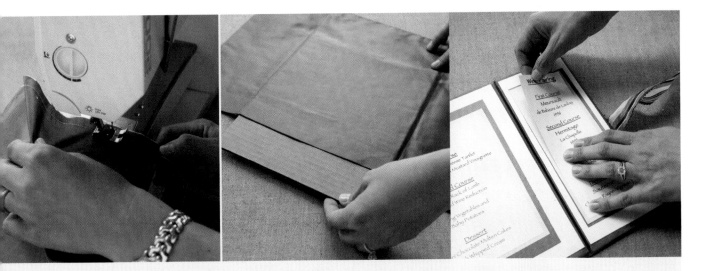

WHAT YOU'LL DO

1. Cut a 16¾ x 10¾-inch paper pattern; this size allows for seams. Pin the pattern to the fabric and cut the fabric.

2. Place the right sides of fabric together then stitch (with a ⅜-inch seam) around top and sides of fabric. Leave the bottom open. Turn fabric inside out—the right side of the fabric will now be facing out. Press fabric with an iron.

3. Holding fabric with open end at the bottom, stitch a seam from top to bottom 4 inches in from each side. This creates three separate areas, each with an opening at the bottom.

4. Cut one piece of cardboard in half vertically. Slide the uncut piece of cardboard into the center pocket. Use the two smaller pieces of cardboard to fill the side pockets. Fold under the bottom seam and use the glue gun to close the seam.

5. Fold sides in and wrap ribbon around entire invitation. Hot glue the ribbon in place at edge of each wing. Tie bow with ribbon and cut off excess.

6. Create the printed portion of the invitation (see card-stock invitation instructions, page 58). Create three separate documents. In the first, set the margin to 5¾ x 7½ inches and type the actual menu, centering the courses on the page. For the other two documents, set the margins to 3¼ x 8½ inches. In the second document type the wines for each course or other information, again centering the text. In the third document, type the actual party invitation using the same format as for the wine-pairing document.

7. Print the three documents on printer-friendly paper. Cut the menu portion to size, approximately 5¼ x 7 inches. Cut the wine and party invitation documents to fit the wings, about 2¾ x 8 inches.

8. Cut three pieces of coordinating paper, one 5¾ x 7½ inches and two 3¼ x 8½ inches. Then cut three pieces of card stock, one 8 x 10 inches and two 4 x 10 inches. Using spray mount adhesive, attach the printed menu to the larger piece of coordinating paper. Repeat, attaching each of the side text pieces to coordinating paper. Use spray mount to attach each two-layer printed piece to the cardstock. Attach the card stock to the fabric-covered board.

project IRON-ON COCKTAIL NAPKIN

How to create an invitation that is clever and different, but still easy to mail? Why not actually print the information for the party right on the kind of napkin you might use at the party, a cocktail napkin as the invitation for a cocktail party or a dinner napkin for a dinner party. I remembered using T-shirt iron-on transfers as a kid and it seemed like a great idea to use them once again for creating unique yet inexpensive invitations.

Cocktail napkins are usually 5 inches square so when typing the invitation, make sure all the information fits in this size square. I usually do not set margins—too much work! Instead I just print a sample on paper first to make sure the text will fit.

WHAT YOU'LL NEED

EQUIPMENT

- Computer and printer
- Iron
- Scissors

MATERIALS

For each invitation:

- 2 sheets iron-on ink-jet printer paper
- 1 cocktail napkin (5 x 5 inches)

WHAT YOU'LL DO

1. Open a new word processing document and type in the invitation details. Select font and format text. Once it is formatted to your liking, flip the text.* Then print a sample on plain paper, making sure the text sample is the right size to fit onto the napkin. If everything is correct, print on the iron-on paper. Trim excess iron-on paper from surrounding text.

2. Place the iron-on paper face down on the napkin and iron in place.** Once cool, peel the back off the transfer.

3. Print image to appear on front of invite onto iron-on paper. Trim excess paper and iron image onto front of napkin. Let cool and peel the back off the transfer.

*If you do not know how to flip text, check your word processing program's help file. Key search words include "mirror text," "flip," or "T-shirt transfer."

**Read the iron-on paper manufacturer's instructions before ironing the image onto fabric.

Keep a copy of the guest list in your Party Planning Journal. That way you'll know who came to which party and can avoid serving the same food to the same people or duplicating the exact mix of guests at another party. It might seem inspired to introduce Monica to Wendy because they're both mad for country music and men in cowboy boots, and it is—once. Ditto your "funny neighbor"—don't subject the same guests to him a second time; torture a new group with his party tricks.

Your journal is also the place for sketches and ideas as you plot out what kind of invitation to make. Stick any color swatches or paper samples here too or post your sources and prices for invitations to buy.

Please join us for a
Wine Tasting
Saturday, September 24th
7:30 pm

Hosted by
Ed & Kimberly Kennedy
R.S.V.P.
404-555-1234

CHAPTER 6

KITCHEN *Confidential*

What shall we eat? That's a big question and one I love to spend time answering. Curled up in my favorite chair with a stack of cookbooks, I look for culinary inspiration and practical recipes. Often I'll plan the food for a party around the look and feel I want the event to have. I love experimenting with different cuisines and will often find inspiration in the unlikeliest of places. Flipping through a travel magazine and seeing some bright cushions on a tiled floor once prompted me to create a Moroccan-inspired party, and I scoured my cookbooks until I found a great couscous recipe. On another occasion my friend Dawn and I planned a girls'-night-in dinner and sleepover party, which we knew was going to be all about fun. Because we wanted a kick-up-your-heels kind of party we chose a vibrant main dish of Island Pork, which is spicy, colorful, and totally delicious. It was a real hit.

You can choose the food first and plan the table accordingly, or you can plan the menu to match the table you've already envisioned. Either way, just bear in mind that selecting a menu for your party is an important step. The more thought and planning you put into your food selections now, the easier the meal will be to make.

COMPOSING THE MENU

You need to know what type of party you're having and how many guests will be coming before you can hone your food choices.

TIME AND COMPLEXITY Make sure the menu includes several recipes that can be made wholly or partially in advance of the day of the party. Many dressings, sauces, soups, one-pot dishes, and desserts can be made a day or two ahead, and sometimes even benefit from resting a day or so before serving. Dishes which call for peeling, chopping, or mincing and other tedious prep work can be partially prepared in advance so that prep and cooking on the day of the party goes much faster. And don't forget the freezer. Foods that freeze well can be made a week or two before your party, freeing up your precious time on the day of the party.

SOMETHING SPECIAL Don't be afraid to try something out of the ordinary. You're inviting guests over, so spice it up a bit and try to serve something a bit different from what they eat at home. That said, whatever menu you choose, try *all* of the recipes out on your family before you serve them to guests. Not only will you be sure the food tastes good, you will also be familiar with the preparation of each recipe so things will go faster and more smoothly. Plus knowing how long recipes take to make will help you in managing your prep time for the party. And, most important, if the recipe turns out to be not so tasty, it's a lot less embarrassing to order pizza for the family than for your dinner guests.

FLAVORS The components of your menu should compliment one another so consider the flavors of each course. Really, a lot of this is common sense. If two flavors seem to go together, they probably do. Aim for a range of flavors from dish to dish. If blue cheese is the main ingredient of one dish, do not use it in another. Similarly, think about the type of flavors; you don't want the menu to be overwhelmingly sweet, rich, or spicy. Find a nice balance for all taste buds.

PRESENTATION Again, variety is key. In addition to tasting good, you want everything to be visually appealing. Select recipes with a variety of colors and textures that will look good together and entertain the mouth. If you make a dish with a white cream sauce as an entrée, don't start the meal with a pale creamy soup.

SEASONALITY Choose dishes that reflect the season and use ingredients that are readily available. Think about it. In August when it's hot and sultry would you rather eat chicken pot pie or grilled fish with tomato salad? In December does a light salad entrée or a hearty pot roast sound better? And as well as matching the food to the season, remember that serving fruit and vegetables when they are in season generally means they are easy to locate, lower in price, and better tasting. (Compare a locally grown peach in June with a peach that flew all the way from Mexico to your grocery store so you could buy it in January.)

ALLERGIES AND SPECIAL DIETS If you know that one of your guests has strict dietary restrictions, whether for health, ethical, or religious reasons, make sure you serve something they can eat. This is particularly true for a sit-down meal. Do not call attention to your friend

by serving him something different—make a meal everyone can eat. However, if you are having a buffet for fifteen and one guest is a vegetarian, don't feel you cannot serve meat to the rest of your company. Just make sure there are plenty of delicious options for vegetarians. Usually at a buffet, I set out small descriptive cards beside each dish listing the name of the dish and any major ingredients or allergens not obvious from the name of the dish. I do this because peanut and shellfish allergies, in particular, can be deadly and you don't want anyone to get sick at your party—nothing ruins the mood of a party like an ambulance.

SUITABILITY Some menus work better for sit-down meals than for buffets. Once you've decided what type of party and how many guests will be coming, make sure the menu you choose suits both of these factors. Some dishes are impossible to eat without being seated at a table. If you are having a buffet remember that few people can navigate meat with bones while holding their plate in their lap, so opt for one-handed food, such as something that is precut on skewers or can be cut with the side of a fork, like pork tenderloin. When you plan your menu, mentally run through how guests will eat it and ensure it is a practical choice.

BUDGET If budget is a consideration, and for most of us it is, make sure you figure the general cost of your meal when you are planning the menu. You don't want any surprises shortly before the day of your event.

ON THE LITTLE BLACK DRESS MENU

It didn't take me long to come up with the entrée for the Little Black Dress Dinner. Lamb is Todd's favorite meat, so it was the obvious choice for a dinner in his honor. Plus lamb isn't something people make at home all that often, so it seems suitably special, especially rack of lamb, which makes such a grand presentation. The vegetables and potatoes are so simple to make, and being so pretty, so little and jewel-like, they will add to the luxurious feel of the meal.

The Cranberry Blue Cheese Tartlet that will be the appetizer is also something Todd likes. You've got to please your audience right—well, at least your guest of honor. His stepmother made the tartlets for his birthday a couple of years

ago and I'd gotten the recipe from her back then. (Never having made them before, I dug out the recipe and tried it in secret.) I'm going to serve the tartlet with mixed greens, as I always like to serve a salad. Plus, the tartlets are quite rich, so the crisp salad will help to balance that out.

For the hors d'oeuvres I wanted something easy that could be made ahead, allowing me to concentrate on the main course on the day of the party and not be worried about trying to fit the hors d'oeuvres into the oven at the last minute. The Smoked Salmon and Dill on Pumpernickel Squares fits the bill perfectly. Not only is it straightforward, but it seems like a big deal, sort of formal.

For dessert, my idea was to do something like a birthday cake but not a birthday cake, something fancy but also fun. Mini-cakes seemed just right. And of course they just had to be chocolate. (Who doesn't love chocolate?) Actually, I'm realizing that both the appetizer tartlets and the dessert suit my haute restaurant meal concept; if you were eating at a four-star place you'd likely get a tartlet or a mini-cake, not a slice cut from a large tart or cake. The individual presentation is so impressive, everyone loves getting his very own thing. You're using the same ingredients; all that's different is the pan. As you can tell, I love to prepare foods that impress the guests without intimidating the hostess!

project LITTLE BLACK DRESS MENU

SPECIALTY DRINK
Panache (Recipe in chapter 7)

HORS D'OEUVRES
Smoked Salmon and Dill on Pumpernickel Squares

APPETIZER
Cranberry Blue Cheese Tartlet and Mixed Greens with Mustard Vinaigrette

MAIN COURSE
Herbed Rack of Lamb with Red Wine Reduction
Glazed Baby Vegetables and Potatoes

DESSERT
Mini Molten Chocolate Cakes with Whipped Cream

RECIPES

SMOKED SALMON AND DILL ON PUMPERNICKEL SQUARES

This recipe is a twist on the classic hors d'oeuvres of smoked salmon slices on pumpernickel bread. I adore that combination but think this is even more irresistible. Plus it's so easy to make; the spread can be made up to two days before the dinner, then everything is assembled just prior to serving so the hors d'oeuvres don't have a chance to dry out.

8 ounces cream cheese, room temperature
3 ounces smoked salmon, cut into $1/2$-inch pieces
1 bunch of fresh dill, sprigs picked from stems
2 to 3 tablespoons heavy cream
Dash of Tabasco sauce

Loaf of small, hors d'oeuvres–size pumpernickel
   bread (or a regular-size loaf of pumpernickel,
   slices cut into 2-inch squares)
2 small radishes, sliced paper thin

1. Place cream cheese, smoked salmon, all but $1/4$ cup of the dill sprigs, 2 tablespoons of cream, and Tabasco sauce in the bowl of a food processor fitted with the metal blade attachment. Blend until smooth and pink with green flecks of dill, adding the reserved tablespoon of cream if the spread seems very stiff.

2. Chill spread for at least 30 minutes or up to 2 days. (If, when you remove the spread from the refrigerator, it is at first too stiff to pipe, let it sit at room temperature for about 10 to 15 minutes.)

3. Place spread in a pastry bag fitted with a small round- or star-shaped tip and pipe mixture onto pumpernickel squares. (A resealable plastic bag with a corner snipped off can also do the work of a pastry bag.)

4. Garnish hors d'oeuvres with one or two slices of radish and a sprig of dill.

Makes about 30 hors d'oeuvres

Serves 8

CRANBERRY BLUE CHEESE TARTLET AND MIXED GREENS WITH MUSTARD VINAIGRETTE

By now you know how I love individual presentations; well if that isn't your thing, you can make this recipe as one large tart and cut slices for each serving. Use one 9-inch tart pan in place of the eight individual tartlets. If you do this you'll only use one half of the pastry, so reserve the other half for another use. (Carefully wrapped in plastic wrap, the dough can be kept in the freezer for up to one month.) Roll out one disc of dough into an 11-inch circle that is about ⅛ inch thick and follow from step #4 on. Remember that this larger shell will take more time to brown and the custard filling will need longer to set.

I adore the mustardy dressing for the greens that accompanies the tartlets; it's so piquant it makes a delicious contrast to the rich custard filling.

FLAKY PASTRY

3 cups unbleached all-purpose flour

1 teaspoon kosher salt

10 ounces (2½ sticks) unsalted butter, chilled and cut into cubes

1. Pulse flour and salt together in the bowl of a food processor fitted with the metal blade attachment. Add the butter to the dry ingredients and pulse until the pieces of butter are pea-sized. With the processor running, drizzle in 7 tablespoons ice water until the dough forms small balls that stick together when pressed. If the dough appears dry and resists sticking together add more ice water, a teaspoon at a time, until the dough comes together.

2. Pour contents of bowl onto a clean work surface and gather dough into a ball. Divide ball in half and press both pieces firmly into flat discs. Wrap snuggly in plastic wrap and refrigerate for at least one hour and up to one day.

3. Roll out one disc of dough into a 12-inch square and cut out four 6-inch circles. Place these rounds on a baking sheet and reserve in the refrigerator while repeating the rolling and cutting with the second disc of dough. Coax each circle of dough into a 4-inch fluted tartlet mold by gently pressing it into the bottom and up the sides of the pan without stretching the dough. Roll the rolling pin firmly across the tops of the tartlet molds so that dough hanging over the edges is trimmed off. Chill dough-lined molds in the freezer for 30 minutes.

4. Preheat the oven to 400°F.

5. Remove molds from the freezer and cover the dough in each with a square of aluminum foil or parchment paper. Fill molds with uncooked rice or beans to weigh down the pastry. Place molds on two baking sheets and bake on the lowest two racks of the oven until pastry shells are an even medium brown, about 20 minutes. Check under foil or parchment to make sure bottom crusts are set and beginning to color. Cool shells in molds and remove foil/parchments and weights.

CRANBERRY CUSTARD FILLING

2 tablespoons olive oil

1 large onion, diced

2 teaspoons kosher salt

1 heaping cup cranberries, fresh or frozen (or $\frac{1}{2}$ cup plump dried cranberries)

1 tablespoon sugar (omit if using dried cranberries)

$\frac{1}{2}$ cup walnuts, toasted

$1\frac{1}{2}$ tablespoons fresh thyme, minced

4 eggs

2 cups heavy cream

4 ounces blue cheese, crumbled

1. Preheat oven to 350°F.

2. Heat oil in a wide, heavy saucepan over medium heat. Add onion and sprinkle with salt. Sauté, stirring frequently and adjusting heat if necessary, until onion is tender and caramelized, about 15 minutes. Add cranberries and sugar and cook until cranberries swell and pop. Stir in walnuts and thyme and set aside to cool.

3. In a bowl, combine eggs and cream; whisk until smooth.

4. Divide walnut-cranberry mixture among the 8 tartlet shells, which should remain in their molds. Sprinkle blue cheese equally over the tops. Pour egg mixture over the filling, taking care to fill them as close to the rim as possible without allowing the custard to spill over the edge.

5. Bake tartlets until custard is set and golden, about 15 minutes.

Makes eight 4-inch tartlets

MIXED GREENS WITH MUSTARD VINAIGRETTE

4 tablespoons Dijon mustard

2 tablespoons red wine vinegar

$\frac{3}{4}$ cup extra-virgin olive oil

$\frac{1}{4}$ cup walnut oil

Salt and pepper to taste

1 pound mixed field greens or mesclun

1. Combine mustard and vinegar in a mixing bowl, stirring until smooth. Combine olive and walnut oils in a liquid measuring cup and slowly drizzle into the mustard/vinegar mixture, whisking until vinaigrette is smooth and emulsified. Season to taste with salt and pepper.

2. Place the salad greens in a very large bowl and add several large spoonfuls of the vinaigrette, pouring it down the sides of the bowl in circular motions. Gently toss the greens until they are generously coated with the vinaigrette, adding one more spoonful at a time as needed. (Reserve remaining vinaigrette in the refrigerator for another use.)

To Serve

Place a generous handful of greens on each salad plate and set the tartlet beside it.

Serves 8

EXPERT TESTIMONY: BEFRIEND THE BUTCHER

Today a lot of people can order sushi with aplomb, tell baby spinach from arugula, and whip up gourmet frozen desserts with their ice cream makers, but they lack confidence about cooking meat and poultry and tend to stick to buying the safest, most expensive cuts. Todd Mussman, chef-owner of Muss & Turner's in Smyrna, Georgia is my local source for the finest meats—as well as cheeses, oils, and condiments—and he shared some tips for overcoming fear of cooking meat.

"Basically," says Mussman, "the best way to become comfortable is to talk to your butcher. Get familiar with different cuts and experiment, buying, cooking, eating, and enjoying them. You might not want to take home a beef shank and trim and braise it yourself, but if you talk to your butcher and tell him what you want to make, even show him a recipe, chances are he'll be able to recommend a cut that's more suitable for you."

CHOOSING WHAT WORKS FOR YOU

"If a recipe calls for a chicken cut into eight pieces, don't abandon the recipe because you don't know how to cut up a chicken; just buy a chicken already cut up or a pack of chicken parts," Mussman recommends.

Chicken tenders cost more than bone-in chicken breasts, just as whole chickens are generally cheaper than a chicken cut into portions. "It's a matter of deciding what you're comfortable doing," Mussman offers.

"Are you ready to cut up that chicken and save a couple of dollars? It really is easy once you get the hang of it. Or would you rather save time by having the meat cut up for you? The choice is yours—as long as you realize you do have a choice."

WORKING IT

If you know you're doing all you can to avoid spreading bacteria, you'll feel more comfortable dealing with meat and poultry. Becoming a scrupulous hand washer is the vital first step to kitchen hygiene. "Wash your hands before you start to handle raw meat or poultry, and be careful to wash them again before going on to prepare the salad or any other part of the meal," Mussman counsels. He suggests keeping one chopping board that is used for only meat and fish. Plastic chopping boards are best for raw meat and fish. Whatever kind of cutting board you use, clean it frequently with hot soapy water. Sanitize both wood and plastic cutting boards with a diluted chlorine bleach solution of one teaspoon of liquid chlorine bleach in one quart of water. Flood the surface with the bleach solution and allow it to stand for several minutes, then rinse and air dry or pat dry with paper towels.

When you're busy cooking for a dinner party, Mussman suggests keeping a bleach water solution (one part bleach to ten parts water) in a small jar together with a clean soft cotton towel or rag on the kitchen counter which can be used to wipe down your board as you work.

Few dishes are as elegant or delicious as a well-prepared rack of lamb and cooking one is far easier than it appears. A rib rack is simply a group of rib chops that has not been separated. When buying a rack, ask the butcher to "French" it, which means asking for the bones on the racks to be scraped clean; many butchers always do this and it gives the racks a cleaner, more spectacular appearance for serving.

HERBED RACK OF LAMB

1 bunch fresh rosemary, needles stripped and coarsely chopped

1 bunch fresh thyme, leaves stripped and coarsely chopped

1 head of garlic, cloves peeled and minced

$\frac{1}{4}$ cup olive oil

3 Frenched lamb racks (each rack should have 8 ribs and weigh $1\frac{1}{2}$ pounds)

1 bunch parsley, picked and coarsely chopped

2 cups dry bread crumbs

8 tablespoons (1 stick) unsalted butter, melted and cooled

Kosher salt and freshly ground pepper

1 cup Dijon mustard

1. In a small bowl combine rosemary, thyme, garlic, and olive oil. Rub herb mixture over the lamb racks, front and back, and place on a baking sheet lined with foil. Cover with plastic wrap and refrigerate overnight.

2. Preheat oven to 450°F. Wipe most of the herb rub off of the lamb racks so it does not burn when the lamb is seared.

3. In a small bowl combine parsley, bread crumbs, and melted butter.

4. Heat olive oil in a large skillet over medium-high heat until it begins to smoke. Working with one rack at a time, place lamb in the pan, fat side down, and sear until brown and caramelized, at least 5 minutes. Turn racks over and quickly sear the other side, it will take only 2 to 3 minutes. Remove racks to a foil-lined baking sheet (with a 1-inch rim all the way around) or roasting pan. Drain fat and oil from skillet after it has cooled, leaving the particulate matter, and set skillet aside.

5. Generously season racks all over with salt and pepper and using a pastry brush or small offset spatula, spread fat-covered side with mustard. Press bread crumb mixture onto the mustard-covered surface, leaving bones exposed.

6. Place racks in the oven and finish cooking by roasting to desired doneness.

7. Roast lamb in oven until meat thermometer inserted into center of lamb registers 130°F for medium-rare, about 20 minutes. Transfer lamb to platter. Let stand 15 minutes before serving.

RED WINE REDUCTION

1 cup dry white wine

4 cloves garlic, minced

$1/4$ cup rosemary, minced

2 cups chicken stock

1 cup low-sodium tomato juice

2 tablespoons unsalted butter

Kosher salt and freshly ground black pepper to taste

1. Place reserved skillet over medium-high heat and when bits of caramelized meat stuck to bottom of pan begin to sizzle, pour in wine, scraping up bits with a wooden spoon.

2. Add garlic, rosemary, stock, and tomato juice. Bring to a boil, lower heat, and simmer until reduced in volume by $3/4$ and about 1 cup of thickened liquid remains.

3. Off the heat, whisk in butter and season to taste with salt and pepper.

GLAZED BABY VEGETABLES AND POTATOES

1 pound small waxy potatoes, peeled and quartered

1 tablespoon salt

$1/2$ pound baby carrots

$1/2$ pound green beans, trimmed

$1/2$ pound frozen peas

3 tablespoons olive oil

$1/2$ pound frozen pearl onions

1 tablespoon sugar

2 tablespoons butter

Kosher salt and freshly ground black pepper

1. Place potatoes in a medium saucepan and cover by 1 inch with cold water. Add a tablespoon of salt and bring to a boil. Cook potatoes in simmering water until they are just tender, about 5 minutes. Drain thoroughly and set aside.

2. Bring a large pot of generously salted water to a boil. Add carrots and green beans and boil for 3 minutes. Add peas and continue to cook at a simmer for 1 more minute. Drain vegetables and set aside.

3. Heat oil in a skillet over medium heat. When oil is shimmering and barely smoking, add potatoes and sauté until golden brown, stirring occasionally to prevent sticking. Add pearl onions, and sugar and sauté until well caramelized. Deglaze with enough water to cover the bottom of the pan,

scraping up the bits of vegetable stuck to the pan as the water simmers rapidly. Add carrots, peas, and green beans and cook through until heated.

4. Reduce heat and add butter, stirring everything together gently until vegetables are coated with the glossy brown glaze. (Add a little water if pan gets too dry.) Season to taste with salt and freshly ground pepper.

To Serve

Slice lamb racks into individual chops and place three chops on each plate. Scatter vegetables around the lamb and spoon sauce over the meat, drizzling some around the vegetables.

Serves 8

These individual chocolate cakes look very sophisticated, taste divine, and make a grand finale to a special dinner. They're made in small Bundt molds that are sold six to a pan at specialty cookware stores such as Williams-Sonoma. They are 6-ounce molds that, unlike traditional Bundt pans, do not have a hole in the center. Eight 6-ounce ramekins may be used in place of the Bundt molds.

Though the cakes can't be baked ahead since they wouldn't be warm and "molten" when eaten, the batter can be made ahead, and divided between the Bundt or ramekin molds.

8 tablespoons (1 stick) unsalted butter

Cocoa powder, sifted

8 ounces semisweet chocolate, chopped

4 large eggs

1 large egg yolk

1 teaspoon pure vanilla extract

1 teaspoon orange or hazelnut liqueur (such as Grand Marnier or Frangelico)

$\frac{1}{2}$ teaspoon salt

$\frac{1}{2}$ cup granulated sugar

2 tablespoons all-purpose flour

Powdered sugar for decoration

Whipped cream or vanilla ice cream for serving

1. Heat oven to 400°F. Using cooled melted butter and a pastry brush, grease the miniature Bundt pans and coat with sifted cocoa powder, knocking them out lightly over the sink to remove any powder that has not adhered to the molds. Line two rimmed baking sheets with parchment paper and place one Bundt pan on each.

2. Melt the remaining butter and chocolate together in a medium-sized heatproof bowl set over a pan of water that has not yet come to a simmer. Make sure the bottom of the bowl is at least several inches above the surface of the water. Stir the mixture gently until smooth and remove bowl from heat. Set aside to cool slightly.

3. Beat eggs, yolk, vanilla, liqueur, salt, and sugar on high speed in the bowl of an electric mixer fitted with a whisk attachment, or with handheld electric beaters, until the volume of the eggs has almost tripled and the mixture is pale yellow and drops from the lifted beaters in thick ribbons. Pour melted chocolate over the egg mixture and using a large rubber spatula, fold in chocolate with as few strokes as possible to avoid deflating the eggs. Sprinkle flour over chocolate mixture and rapidly fold in with a light hand.

4. Using a small ladle or an ice-cream scoop, fill the 8 prepared molds. (At this stage they can be covered with plastic wrap and refrigerated for several hours. Let sit out on the counter for a half hour or so before baking.)

5. Bake cakes, one sheet at a time, in the center of the oven until they have risen about a half-inch above the tops of the molds; they will have a top crust, though their centers will still appear a bit glossy and will jiggle slightly when the pan is slid back and forth, about 12–14 minutes. (Baking times will vary depending on the molds and oven used. Underbaking is preferable to overbaking.)

6. Run a paring knife around the inside edges of the molds and invert them onto a large piece of parchment paper sitting on the counter. Allow to cool for a minute, then lift off Bundt pan.

Transfer the cakes to individual serving plates and dust with powdered sugar. Serve with a dollop of whipped cream.

Makes 8 individual cakes

JOURNAL ENTRY

Recipes tend to come from a variety of sources and can easily be misplaced or lost, so photocopy all your recipes and keep the copies in your Party Planning Journal. Even if you find an entire menu in a magazine or cookbook and want to reproduce it for your party, make a copy and keep it in your journal so you have it on hand and can refer to the menu and recipes when planning future parties.

FROM *Cocktails* TO *Coffee*

CHAPTER 7

Ah, drinks. I consider them hospitality at its most essential. What's the first thing you do for a guest after you greet her and take her coat? You get her a drink. Maybe it's a comfort thing, but I think people feel naked if they don't have a glass in hand at a party. It can be a glass of Champagne or seltzer or not even a glass, but a bottle of beer. Whatever the beverage, holding it makes a guest feel as if she is officially part of the party.

Most events offer some sort of alcohol, but don't settle for the same old, same old. Get creative with your drink choices. Whether you want to serve fruity lemonade, the finest teas, one wine, a selection of wines, or a signature cocktail, the possibilities are endless.

I always serve wine at dinner parties. Sometimes one wine before dinner as an aperitif and a different one to complement the food during the meal. For very special dinners, I pair a different wine with each course. However you may want to serve wine at your party, consider trying something unusual or unexpected. Try different varieties of wine and experiment with wine and food pairings.

And don't forget coffee and tea. As well as being essential for a brunch or afternoon tea, they strike the right endnote after a delicious dinner, and for a larger party, bringing out coffee and tea signals that the party is winding down.

Why don't you slip out of that wet bathing suit and

The Glass Is Half Full

If you look at etiquette books from the fifties you'll see drawings of highballs, Collins, old-fashioned, and cordial glasses. To be a gracious hostess back then meant serving a drink in the correct glass. Heaven help the hostess who offered a Rum Collins in a highball. What a breach of decorum! She would have been the talk of the local ladies club for weeks after. Luckily today things are more casual and relaxed. A purist may still assert that a martini is best in a martini glass, but many tony bars serve martinis in other types of glasses just to be different. No reason you can't do the same. All you really need are all-purpose glasses, either short juice-type tumblers, which are great for juice, scotch and soda, or even wine, or taller "highball" glasses, which work well for everything from beer to Bloody Marys or lemonade.

Wine is generally my drink of choice, and I can recognize the different styles of wineglasses made especially for Riesling or Burgundy. I don't use region-specific glasses myself, though I do use wineglasses for red and white wine, and of course, given my love for Champagne, I have flutes. Having stemmed wineglasses is great, but don't get stuck on the glasses you use for wine service: remember that in French bistros and Italian trattorias wine is often served in tumblers that are a lot like juice glasses and that seems just fine. Drink wine to enjoy it, not to impress others.

into a dry martini: ROBERT BENCHLEY

SIGNATURE DRINKS

A signature cocktail can add a distinctive touch to a party. By signature cocktail I mean a creative drink that's not too sweet, not too sour, and not a strong mixed drink. Serving a drink that people haven't tried before adds an element of fun and surprise and can really give your party an air of celebration. (A signature drink can also help you stick to your budget. Instead of trying to shake up an entire bar's worth of liquor, you limit the choices to your special drink and maybe one wine or beer, juice, and soda. Then you don't have to stock up on a full bar—and who has the time, cash, or space to do that?) Check out some of the cocktail recipe books around these days and mix up the drinks that take your fancy. A word of caution, though. Just as you need to try and taste all the food before the party, you need to make sure a drink is as good as it sounds. But trying different drinks is fun and I'm sure you can find a friend or two willing to help you out. . . . And while you're at it, be sure to try some unusual juices or sodas so that your nonalcoholic drink choices are as interesting as the boozy ones.

A signature drink is usually served before a meal, at which time everyone moves to wine, beer, water, or soda for dinner. Nevertheless, a signature drink should complement the menu, theme, and season—no tomato martinis in January please. Consider the practicality of your signature drink; a cocktail that will keep you busy behind the bar for the entire evening is not practical. You want to be out there mingling with guests, not behind the bar wiping your brow. Choose a drink that's relatively simple to prepare. If you decide to serve a drink that takes more prep time, try one that can be made in advance. If you're hosting a large number of guests, choose something that can be made in big batches so you can keep the drinks flowing. My make-ahead favorite is sangria (see recipe, page 97). Perhaps Spain's most famous drink after sherry, sangria is a red wine punch that actually improves over time and tastes so relaxed, so fruity and fun.

PANACHE

This is my all-time favorite drink and it's become my signature. I love Champagne and this cocktail is all about the bubbly, with just a hint of almond. Plus it has a great presentation. The cinnamon stick is more than just an attractive garnish; the Champagne bubbles travel up the cinnamon stick and infuse the drink with spice. The Panache is sophisticated—with a twist. It's been a great hit with everyone I've made it for.

2 bottles (750 ml) Champagne, chilled
1½ cups (12 tablespoons) Torani Italian Almond syrup*
12 Cinnamon sticks

1. Fill glass ⅔ full with Champagne.
2. Pour 1 tablespoon almond syrup into each glass.
3. Place cinnamon stick in glass and serve.
Makes 12 drinks

*Torani Italian syrups are available at gourmet grocery shops, Torani.com, or at stores such as World Market. Other brands of almond syrup will work in this recipe.

TOASTY

A sophisticated cocktail that gets its name because it makes you feel kind of warm and cozy, the Toasty is grown-up, but comfortable. I'm really not a liquor drinker but I can't resist this nutty, kind of toasty flavor. And I love the creamy café au lait color!

1 ounce vodka, chilled

1 ounce Kahlúa

1 ounce Frangelico

1 ounce half-and-half

1 cup ice

1. Combine all ingredients in a shaker.

2. Shake well and strain into a glass.

Makes 1 drink

Note: If your shaker is large enough, this recipe can be scaled up and four Toasties can be made at the same time.

When I don't want to serve wine I often make Sangria. It's particularly delicious on a long hot summer's day. I've tried many different recipes and this is my all-time favorite version.

3 oranges, sliced

3 green apples, cored and sliced

3 bunches seedless green grapes

4½ ounces brandy (Optional)

3 cups orange juice

6 tablespoons super-fine sugar

3 bottles (750 ml) inexpensive light red wine, such as Rioja, chilled

36 ounces club soda, chilled

Ice

1. Combine orange and apple slices and grapes in a large pitcher.

2. Add the brandy, orange juice, and sugar, and stir until the sugar has dissolved.

3. Slowly pour in wine.

4. Refrigerate for at least 2 hours.

5. When ready to serve, add club soda and ice.

Serves 16

Drink Sense

No matter what drink selection you offer, be sure to stock up on bottled water, soda, and juices for designated drivers and others who want non-alcoholic options. Think of the safety of your guests and others. Make certain that the amount of alcohol offered at your party is more than compensated for by the amount of food available. If you notice a guest has had too much to drink, arrange a lift home for him, or offer your guest room or couch.

WINE

I get my love of wine from my parents. They taught me a lot about enjoying wine, about being sensible about drinking, and never being a wine snob. When I hear someone putting on or boasting about some fancy wine, or wine he thinks is fancy, I want to shout "It's just grape juice for goodness sake."

It really is all about the grape. The grapes classified as white range in color from a pale green to shades of yellow into light brown. The juice squeezed from these grapes will be some shade of pale yellow, maybe with a hint of green. The color comes from the grape skin, so the longer the skin is in contact with the juice, the darker the resulting color of the wine. Since white wine generally has the skins,

It's all about the grape.

pulp, stems, and other debris removed early, its color is light. The wine doesn't produce a sediment, which will settle to the bottom, so it can be sold in a clear glass bottle, though many winemakers choose to use green glass bottles.

The grapes classified as red range in color from shades of red into very dark purple. If grape skins are removed early in the process, the resulting wine, such as blush, has a lighter color because the juice from a red grape is a pale yellow. Most red wine is made for maximum color so fermentation occurs with the solids in contact. Sediment will eventually form in the bottle, and sunlight will harm quality, so reds come in dark green bottles, or, in Italy, brown bottles.

EXPERT TESTIMONY: DECODING A WINE LABEL

There's a dizzying amount of information crammed onto the two small labels on every bottle of wine. What does it all mean? How can it help you to choose a wine that suits your palate and the meal you're planning?

"Wine makers are trying to express their ideas and opinions about their wine and wine making on these small spaces," explains Robert Chapman, director of wine at The Grape in Atlanta. He emphasizes that while the information on the label is nowhere near as important as how the wine tastes to you, nevertheless, reading the label carefully can provide you with some useful information about the wine inside.

Most wine bottles have two labels. The front label is eye-catching with creative type and often a distinctive image, anything from a drawing of the chateau where the wine was produced to the handprint of the wine maker's baby, or even a painting by a world-renowned artist. American law requires that the front label contain the type of wine (this means table wine, sparkling wine, or dessert wine); the alcohol content, which is generally between 11 and 13 percent (or if the wine is labeled "table wine" less than 14 percent); and the name and address of the bottler, which may or may not be the same as the wine's producer, and the country of origin.

Law also dictates other information that must appear, but not necessarily on the front label:

How much wine is in the bottle: which is expressed in milliliters; a standard wine bottle is 750 ml, which translates as 25.6 ounces.

Contains sulfites: "Sulfites are a natural preservative used for wine," says Chapman. "Very few wines have no preservatives and some that do not contain sulfites may use a different, more harsh preservative."

Brand name: anything from someone and son proprietor, to a major company with a recognizable name.

Government warning: Every bottle must include a warning about the dangers of drinking alcohol.

Once they've included all the required information, wineries can tell you a lot of other details about what's inside the bottle, or they can spin a seductive story about the wine itself. The type of detail found on the back label varies widely, from simply the importer's name and ad-

dress, to the story behind the vineyard, to information on what foods they recommend pairing their wine with.

Varietal: U.S. wines usually state the grape varietal on the front label, i.e., the type of grape used for the wine, which Chapman notes is a particularly American trait. To be labeled Zinfandel or Pinot Noir a wine must contain a minimum of 75 percent of that particular grape. French, Italian, and Spanish wines all include information on what area the wine was produced in, rather than, or more frequently than, the type of grape used. "Think of Champagne," he suggests. "You know it comes from the Champagne region of France but you probably don't know what grapes were used to make it."

Estate-bottled: means the company that grew the grapes also bottled the wine.

Reserve: used to indicate a "more special bottle," remarks Chapman. It may mean the winery considers this wine came from the best fruit or was made with more expensive wine-making processes. It also suggests you'll pay more for this wine than its nonreserve relation.

Vintage date: the year the grapes were harvested. This is the vintage year even if the wine was not bottled until a year or more later. If a wine is a blend of multiple vintages then no date will be specified.

project DRESS UP YOUR DRINK

Who ever guessed that wine charms would be so popular? Maybe it's because they are both pretty and practical. Each charm is unique, so can be used to identify your glass, which beats trying to recognize it from the shade of lipstick on the rim. I've made charms to suit the themes or style of many different parties, often using materials as simple as card stock, raffia, and a rubber stamp.

Beaded wine charms really are the classic of the genre and this is my take on them. Using the wire hoop earring simplifies the process and creates a charm that is easy to slip on and off a wine glass.

WHAT YOU'LL NEED

EQUIPMENT

- Needle-nose pliers

MATERIALS

For each wine charm you'll need:

- Glass beads
- Silver beads
- Wire hoop earring, 1-inch diameter
- Charm

WHAT YOU'LL DO

1. String half of beads onto wire hoop in desired order. Place charm on hoop.

2. Continue stringing beads until wire is full. Bend $\frac{1}{16}$-inch kink in end of wire so it will lock at loop hole.

NONALCOHOLIC DRINKS

Consider serving a nonalcoholic signature drink. My favorite nonalcoholic cocktail is the Baby Bellini (see recipe, page 103), a little something I whipped up for my friend Andrea's baby shower. I wanted to serve a drink that tasted good and seemed truly festive so that the mom-to-be wouldn't feel like she was missing out. Bubbles are celebratory, so what could be better than a take on the Bellini, a classic Champagne and peach purée drink? I also love sparkling punches and usually serve them in a frozen ice ring made using a Bundt pan as an ice mold, so the punch looks really spectacular. Whether you have a special nonalcoholic drink or not you should always offer a selection of nonalcoholic beverages in addition to alcoholic options. What you serve depends on what you and your guests like and what type of party you are hosting. I offer bottled sparkling water, an assortment of sodas, and keep a six-pack of nonalcoholic beers around so those who cannot drink alcohol will not feel or look out of place around those who are drinking.

The first time I made these delicious nonalcoholic drinks, they were a big success—the guest of honor had at least four! For twelve guests I'd prepare the exact recipe below; it can be halved or otherwise divided for a different number of guests. For twelve guests, it's likely that the fourth bottle would remain in the refrigerator but it's always better to have more than you need plus the cider keeps for a long time. If you have time and ripe peaches are in season, pit, peel, and purée peaches to make the sweetest of all peach purées.

$1^{1}/_{2}$ cups peach concentrate, chilled*

4 bottles (750 ml bottle) sparkling cider such as
   Martinelli's, chilled

48 raspberries**

1. Pour 1 tablespoon peach concentrate into each glass.

2. Fill each Champagne glass two-thirds full with sparkling cider.

3. Drop 2 raspberries into each Champagne flute and serve.

Makes 24 drinks

---

*If you cannot find peach concentrate or purée, buy frozen peaches and purée.

**Raspberries are generally sold in either $^{1}/_{2}$-pint or 6-ounce packages, you'll need more than one $^{1}/_{2}$ pint or one package for this recipe.

THE PERFECT MATCH

Remember when pairing food and wine, the goal is synergy and balance. One should not overpower the other. The best way to work out what goes together is to try a certain wine with a certain dish. But before you buy a bottle to sample with your pâté or pasta, here are some general guidelines to keep in mind.

Pair lighter-bodied wines with lighter food, a Sauvignon Blanc with fresh goat cheese for instance, and fuller-bodied wines like Shiraz with heartier, more flavorful dishes such as steak au poivre.

Think beyond Chardonnay. There really is a whole world of wines out there so try something different. Ask for advice at your local wine store, you'll find the staffers enjoy sharing their knowledge. Tell them how much you'd like to spend and whether you want to taste something you haven't tried before or you want a wine to go with a particular dish; either way they will be happy to help.

If you plan to pair different wines with different courses at a dinner, consider this: light-bodied before heavy, dry before sweet, and low alcohol before high. That usually means white wines first, then reds, and finally dessert wines, whether red or white, with dessert (surprise!).

MATCHING WINE WITH FOOD

Remember these are guidelines; any pairing is fine, as long as you enjoy it.

Type of Food

Salty snacks, smoked fish

Smoked salmon, caviar, or raw oysters

Spicy or smoked dishes

Barbecue

Thai food with coconut

Spicy Thai food

Strongly flavored fish

Tuna, swordfish, mackerel,
   bluefish, grilled salmon

Rich dishes

Beef/steak

Hard cheese

Parmesan

Creamy Cheese and Sauces

Brie

Pasta

Red sauce

Tangy white sauce

Delicate white sauce

Clam or other seafood sauce

Desserts

Creamy and/or fruity desserts

Chocolate

Type of Wine

Sparkling wines

Champagne, Prosecco, or Californian Sparkling wine

Fruity low-alcohol wines

Zinfandel, Beaujolais, Valpolicella

Gewürztraminer, Viognier

Reisling

Fruity reds

Pinot Noir, Malbec, Merlot

Full-bodied classic red wines

Cabernet, Merlot, Rhône reds, Shiraz

Medium-bodied wines

Chianti, Barolo

Medium-bodied white wines

Chardonnay

Match the wine to the sauce

Dry red: Chianti, Montepulciano, Barolo

Chardonnay

Sauvignon Blanc

Frascati, Pinot Grigio

Sweet (dessert) wines

Sauternes

Muscat

BUBBLES AND MORE

It has to be Champagne.

Champagne makes an event so special it was such an obvious choice for this Little Black Dress Dinner Party. Besides, it's my favorite drink. (Luckily Todd likes it too.) I could just serve lovely Champagne, but decided to turn it into a signature drink in the form of Panache. Not everyone has had Panache before and it's such a lively drink I know everyone would enjoy it.

The wines for the evening took a bit more thought. As you've probably realized, I'm a real wine enthusiast—but never a wine snob. I thought this meal was the perfect opportunity to pull out something extra extra good. Great wine doesn't have to be reserved for that rare occasion. There's no reason you can't drink a bottle of pricey wine on a Friday night with your best friend and a take-out pizza. Still, I thought this meal was a reason to indulge, so I wanted to find something suitably grand. At some point, I can't remember when, I figured the wines should be French. Maybe it was playing off that fancy restaurant idea. (Many of the poshest restaurants tend to be French.) Anyway, there are many excellent French wines at all price points, so I wasn't really narrowing my selections by thinking that. My first decision was the stand-out wine, an Hermitage, a powerful red Rhône. I was lucky enough to find a really wonderful one. It wasn't cheap, but sometimes you just have to go all out. If I hadn't gone with that I might have chosen a good Californian Cabernet Sauvignon.

Once I'd chosen that red I needed to consider what wine to serve with the appetizer tartlet and salad. I could serve a light red wine like a Beaujolais, but somehow it seems more suitable to start with white wine and white wine glasses, then change to red and red wine glasses with the lamb. I guess it makes more of a show, and more of a show of that Hermitage I'm so looking forward to drinking. In the end I chose a Meursault, which is what I'd call a nutty and grainy kind of bold white wine. Since we are going to have such a big wine with the lamb I felt we needed a stronger white, not a delicate or very dry wine like a sauvignon blanc. Something with more pants! Otherwise there is just too much of a leap from one wine to the other.

As this is a pull out all the stops event, I want to serve a dessert wine as well. I love how the table looks with all those glasses—white wine, red wine, dessert wine, and water goblets—gathered at each place. In keeping with the French wine theme, I chose a Sauternes. But, as dessert wine is harder to choose than other wines (some inexpensive dessert wines can taste like cough syrup), and as Sauternes can vary greatly, I thought it best to ask for advice from my local wine merchant, who recommended a nice selection that suited my budget.

PLAYING BARTENDER

For larger parties such as buffets, BBQs, or cocktails, you may want to set up a self-service bar. When I have a buffet party I make the beverages buffet style too, which is easy on the guests, and less work for me. Consider what type of beverages you are going to offer and what your guests usually drink. You really don't need to stock as much as a com-

Warm drinks at a couple of parties have taught me not to depend on the ice to chill drinks. Drinks to be served cold need to be refrigerated first then transferred to ice to keep them chilled.

mercial bar. If you have vodka, bourbon or whiskey, maybe gin or rum, and plenty of mixers and juices plus wine and beer, you're well stocked.

For a self-service bar, I uncork the white wine and set it in an ice bucket. You don't need a fancy silver ice bucket for wine, and something bigger is definitely better for chilling lots of beer or soda. I enjoy choosing something a little different to ice my drinks in. A galvanized tub or even a potting tub works fine. A landscaping store can be the perfect spot to find just the right inexpensive item. Sometimes I spray-paint the tub to match the look of the party. Make sure whatever you choose is large enough but not oversized or you'll have to buy loads of extra ice just to fill the bucket. Be sure to check that it doesn't sweat or it could mark your table or floor.

I arrange wineglasses and large highball-type glasses (they're right for just about any drink that doesn't belong in a wineglass) on a circular tray on the table. The tray loosens up the look of the glasses so they aren't in regimented lines. If a signature drink is on the menu, I will make a pitcherful or set out the necessary ingredients with a card listing directions for mixing nearby. If I'm serving bottles of mineral water I'll cool them in ice buckets along with the soda, or I'll put out a pitcher of ice water and some water glasses on the bar. Cocktail napkins and sliced lemons and limes are also essentials. And don't forget a bottle opener.

If you can afford to hire a bartender, do so for a really big blowout event; it's an expense you won't regret. I rarely hire any assistance when I host parties, even when the guest list exceeds seventy-five people, but I have hired a bartender on at least three occasions. As long as you are not offering full bar service and shaking martinis and all kinds of cocktails, a bartender without extensive experience will suit just fine. For my parties, I hire local college boys. They are cheaper than a professional bartender, yet, for my purposes, do as good a job. Besides, the college boys are so cute—it's like having an extra treat for my female guests and me. A little eye candy never hurts a party!

BREWING UP

Which is worse, bad coffee or no coffee? For a hostess, coffee is simple—you already know how to make it—but vital. Make some to accompany dessert, perk up designated drivers, or signal to stragglers that the time to leave is soon. Offer both caffeinated and decaf brews so those who love the taste but cannot handle the caffeine, particularly at night, can indulge. Tea also has many fans so keep a couple of caffeinated teas, black tea such as English Breakfast and Earl Grey or a green tea like jasmine, and some herbal varieties like basic mint or chamomile or more exotic fruit-flavored ones around for those who like to end a meal with a calming cuppa.

I love the ritual and elegance of making a pot of tea, as well as the taste of the tea sipped from a pretty tea cup or my favorite mug. And it's useful to be able to make a good pot of tea for tea-drinking friends when other guests are having coffee after dinner. If you grew up in a household where everyone drank coffee or iced tea and only encountered hot tea made in a mug or cup with a tiny tea bag, using loose tea and a teapot can seem intimidating, but it's easy, as Michael Harney, tea buyer of Harney & Sons Tea Company, explains.

BLACK TEA

1. Filter the water.

"The Chinese say water is the mother of tea so you have to use good water for your tea," advises Harney. "Tap water generally contains chlorine or some other elements that will adversely affect the taste of the tea, so run it through a water filter."

2. Boil the water. Get it as close to 212°F. as possible.

"Most Americans drink black tea, which requires boiling water (for green tea, see page 110). The water should be brought to the boil then used to make the tea, not kept at a boil."

3. Preheat the pot by swirling a little boiling water in it. Then pour out the water.

"Most teapots are a little chilly to the touch, and if you pour the boiling water into the cool pot you loose a lot of its temperature. So do as the Brits do," Harney counsels, "and warm the pot."

4. Add one teaspoon of tea per cup to the pot and pour boiling water over the tea leaves. Leave to steep for about five minutes.

The length of time the tea takes to brew depends on the type of tea used (most packages will have brewing guidelines). It's also a matter of personal taste.

5. Pour the tea through a strainer and serve with milk and sugar if desired.

Some teapots have built in strainers or come with removable strainers or use a separate strainer that rests on top of your cup.

HERBAL TEA

Follow the steps for black tea, steeping according to type of herbal tea used.

GREEN TEA

Follow the steps for black tea but do not boil the water. The water should be no hotter than 180ºF, and do not preheat the pot. Let the tea steep for 1–3 minutes (depending on the type of green tea used) before serving/pouring.

"Green tea requires less temperature and less time," says Harney. "Brewed correctly, many green teas can be sweet; bitter tastes come out in tea that is oversteeped." Also note that green tea is not generally served with milk or sugar.

Journal Entry

Make a list of the wines you'll be serving and keep it in your journal so you can remember what you want to buy (or not) for future parties. Also keep the recipe for any specialty drink you're making here so you can refer to it easily now and find it later when you want to make it for another party.

CHAPTER 8

This Way
PLEASE

Preparing your home for entertaining involves more than the vacuum and the feather duster. Cleanup is essential, but more important than evicting those dust bunnies is actually orchestrating the party. Defining the party space, organizing where the main events of the party will occur—where party-goers will be served food and drink, where they will eat and talk, where gifts will be opened, or games played—is vital. So is planning how best to set up food and drink so that people can move freely around the bar and the buffet, creating areas that encourage conversation. The more guests you invite, the more you have to think about it. That's common sense. But even for a small dinner party you need to make sure there is enough room for everyone to move about freely, enough chairs for guests to sit on, and enough flat surfaces for them to put down their drinks. It's all about making the most of your space—with a bit of cleaning thrown in.

FLOW

How many times have you got caught in a bottleneck at the end of the buffet table? Your plate is full and all you want to do is escape to that last remaining seat on the other side of the room, but you can't because you're hemmed in by other guests who are waiting patiently for their turn with the shrimp and chicken. If that has happened to you, you were a victim of poor "flow."

Flow is all about time and motion. It's about organizing the party space for the best available movement so that your guests can travel about the room, mingling comfortably without having to worry where to stand or sit, or how to reach the dip on the other side of the table. It's also about paying attention to the rhythms of the event so that no one is standing around waiting for the party to begin. Flow is the invisible but essential part of a party that comes about when you've surveyed your room in advance for the best possible movement of people and arrangement of furniture. Good flow occurs when you've planned your party so that everything happens on an unseen schedule. It enables people to move freely and provides plenty of places for them to stop, sit, chat, and eat. It eliminates chaos and gives a party an appealing feel. Bad flow occurs when you haven't given yourself enough time to plan or when the buffet is only accessible from one side and not laid out to allow guests to get their food and make a clean escape. Guests never notice when the flow of a party is good, only when it isn't.

It is the simple things in life

CROWD CONTROL

One of the best preparations for a party is to run through the event in your head. Visualize everything from the moment you greet guests at the door to the time when you wish them good night. Doing this helps you to be aware of the elements you'll need to organize and the spaces you'll need to clear. You'll want to be prepared for all aspects of the party, from where your guests will put their coats, to where they can sit, to where they will be able to find favors as they leave.

Be clear in your head about where the party is to take place. Will guests range over your entire home? Will you want to confine the party to the downstairs level, or concentrate people in the dining room, family room, and kitchen, making sure that no one goes into the study because that's where you intend to deposit all the junk you remove from the party rooms? Having clear parameters for the party is practical in that it keeps people and mess out of certain areas of your home. Not only that, keeping people corralled in a certain area will help you to better gauge if your guests need anything. Simply closing doors or roping off staircases is a good signal to guests to stay out of those rooms and areas.

Keep in mind that even if you place just two chairs around a small table where drinks and food can be set, what you're doing is suggesting a welcoming, comfy spot for party-goers to gather. And they will.

hat are the most extraordinary. PAULA COELHO

SETTING THE STAGE

As you plan what the pros call the "staging areas"—where the party action will take place—consider everything from getting drinks to eating dessert and dancing. Some people find it helpful to do a walk-through as they visualize their party. For a larger gathering such as a drinks party or shower, you may decide you need to edit down the furniture in your main party room to make ample room for guests to mingle without bumping into armchairs or bureaus. Do this now because you certainly don't want to be moving furniture around once your guests arrive.

It might not be practical to provide seating for all twenty guests—at many parties people stand and chat, even stand and eat a three-course meal—so be sure there are surfaces like open tables where guests can rest plates and glasses. Even if you think the party will work better if you take the couch out to make more space, you should always provide some seating. A room emptied of all its chairs does not look inviting. Seating does not have to be big cushy armchairs, though; small folding chairs are fine. And remember: you don't need to buy furniture for a party. Just use what you have to its best advantage.

TAKE A POWDER

Don't forget the powder room. Every guest will likely pay it at least one visit during your party. If you have time to clean only one room then make it the bathroom. No one is likely to notice a few specks of dirt in other rooms but the bathroom, that's where people focus. So make it sparkle and treat guests to some special touches.

In addition to cleaning the bathroom, dress it up for the party with the following:

- new bars of pretty soap
- fresh towels
- tissues
- scented hand cream
- candles (lit for party)
- extra rolls of toilet paper stored in an obvious spot

CONSIDER YOURSELF AT HOME

Hosting a dinner party means most of the action for my event will take place in the dining room. If I were having a buffet meal I'd be working out the flow around the buffet and drinks table and how many seats I needed in the family room. With a dinner party I already know where everyone will be sitting and that I have enough space and chairs at the dining table. My table is large enough to accommodate eight as it is; if it were smaller I'd be adding a leaf right now.

Before dinner we'll have drinks and hors d'oeuvres gathered around the breakfast bar. That's where I usually put the predinner snacks and drinks, but I do need to check that there is enough room for all the glasses, the fixings for the Panache cocktail, and platters of hors d'oeuvres and think how to set out the ingredients for the cocktail so it looks inviting. I always plan all these things through right now, about three weeks before the party, so I'm not in a mess at the last minute.

Luxury must be comfortable, otherwise it's not luxury. COCO CHANEL

MAKING SPACE

If you plan to hide things you clear from the main party area in a closet, be sure to leave space in your coat closet and have some spare hangers waiting for guests' coats. If you don't have a coat closet then do as generations of hostesses have and use your bed. It really doesn't matter where you put coats and purses, it's just important that you think it through and have a place set aside.

When there is a guest of honor and guests are likely to bring gifts, set up a small table where guests can set presents when they arrive. A clean plain tabletop is fine or you can dress the table with a pretty cloth and flowers or flag it with an attractive themed centerpiece like the Rose Box (see page 158). Make it obvious what the table is for by putting your personal gift there first.

If you're having a cocktail party, consider where the bar should be set up. Make sure it is easily accessible and plan to set it up like a buffet, starting with glasses, then ice, then drinks so there is a progression down the table. Set the bar apart from the food table so that someone going for more sangria will not get caught up in the crush around the crudités—people do tend to gather and linger around the chips and dips. One easy way to avoid drinks and food logjams is to place the hors d'oeuvres around the party space rather than concentrating them on one table. Put some on your kitchen table, island, bar, and coffee table.

For a buffet, consider the same traffic flow factors. If you can, set up the buffet so people can serve themselves from both sides of the table. Also think about where you will put the plates, flatware, and napkins; they should be close to the food.

Whatever type of party you're throwing, you need to plan for places for used glasses and plates. People will put dirty glasses in what seems like a logical place to them; if they see plates on a surface they'll stack theirs in the same place, or if they see an open table they'll park their plates on it. And for larger parties, place a garbage can somewhere near—but not too near—the food.

Don't worry if moving your furniture for better flow has left "dimples" in your carpet. Just rub an ice cube over the indentation and the nap will return in a matter of minutes.

project EXTRA LARGE BUFFET TABLE

If you'd like to host a buffet but none of your tables or countertops seem large enough to hold the feast you're planning, why not construct a table? This project makes a 4 x 8-foot table, large and sturdy enough to display a generous spread. For a smaller buffet table, ask the lumber yard to cut the plywood to the size you want. Buy the two card tables at a discount store, make and use the table then fold it away and store the elements in a closet or the basement until the next party.

WHAT YOU'LL NEED

EQUIPMENT

• Hammer

MATERIALS

• 2 folding card tables, each about 33 inches square or 2 sturdy saw horses
• 4 x 8 piece of ¾-inch plywood
• 12 yards of inexpensive fabric such as burlap
• 50 flat tacks
• Tablecloth

WHAT YOU'LL DO

1. Open card tables and lock legs in place.

2. Place the two card tables together.

3. Rest the sheet of plywood on top of the card tables, centering card tables underneath the plywood.

4. Starting at back of the buffet table, place top edge of fabric against edge of plywood and attach fabric to plywood with flat tacks, spacing them about 6 inches apart.

5. Once you have tacked the fabric all the way around, leave 6 extra inches of overlap, then cut off the remaining fabric.

6. Fold the 6 inches of fabric in half (to hide the rough edge of fabric) and tack in place. Trim fabric to desired length or simply tuck any excess fabric under the table.

7. Place tablecloth on top, making sure cloth is large enough to hang over the table edge and cover tacks.

SPRUCING UP

You have to clean the house before everyone comes over, right? It's hard not to think that everything needs to be spotless. I used to really go crazy cleaning before a party but then I realized that I never notice if someone else's house is clean and none of my guests were taking a Q-tip to my baseboards. Seriously you shouldn't spend too much time and energy making every room spotless. You want to make sure your home is picked up and any extraneous items are tidied away; the less cluttered everything looks, the better. Pay particular attention to the bathroom—I do notice if someone's bathroom is less than sparkling—and the kitchen where the lights are bright and people pop in to help themselves to an extra hors d'oeuvre. If you are having a sit-down meal, the dining room should be pretty clean as that is where guests will spend most of their time, but really there's no need to dust. Make a quick pass with the vacuum but keep it in perspective; by the time the first five guests arrive no one will be looking at the carpet. And remember, during the party, lights will be dimmed and guests hopefully will be busy laughing and chatting, not checking out the dust on your CD collection.

PREPARING THE SPACE

- Run through the party you're planning in your head—decide which rooms will be used and which will be closed off.
- Plan where the bar and food will be laid out and consider how to maximize traffic flow around them.
- Plan staging areas and conversation areas and decide what you need to do to prepare these areas. Do you need to move, remove, or add furniture?
- Clear out a coat closet or reserve another space for guests' coats.
- Set up a gift table (if required).
- Organize a place for favors (if using).
- Clean bathroom and organize bathroom supplies for party.
- Clean kitchen.
- Tidy away clutter; put away superfluous items, piles of magazines, mail, CDs, clothing.

Journal Entry

For a cocktail party or buffet, stand in the room where the bar and food will be and make a quick sketch of the room showing where the buffet and bar will be. It doesn't need to be artistic, but it will help to remind you of how to lay things out when you come to set up the tables for the party.

CHAPTER 9

IN THE

Mood

To me the atmosphere of a party is more important than the drinks you pour or the food you serve, or any other element for that matter. Your guests will absorb the ambience, or atmosphere, you create, whether they know it or not.

That's why you want to create a mood that is comfortable and welcoming. So how do you do this? Lighting, candles, music, flowers, and themed decorations might seem like small elements, but together these details help create the right ambience.

A PATH OF LIGHT

Like most elements of a party, lighting is not something to leave to the night of the event, but should be worked out ahead of time. One night when the sun has gone down, experiment with the lights in the rooms where the party will take place. See which combination and intensity of lights create the warmest atmosphere. If you don't already have them, consider putting some dimmers on your lights. Dimmers make possible any degree of light—from super-bright operating-theater level, to complete darkness—and they allow you to adapt the lighting in the living room, dining room, even the bathroom if you choose. Most hardware stores carry dimmers that require no wiring and will work on floor lights or table lights.

Lighting should match the mood of the event: brighter for a dance party than a buffet, brighter for a buffet than a formal sit-down dinner. Try this as a general guide: if you can read a book but would find it somewhat tiring to read several chapters, the light is about right.

Up lighting is more flattering than down lighting. Down lighting is any light that emits from the ceiling, so try table lamps, floor lamps, and candles to provide the most light—that's up lighting—and use ceiling lights sparingly. Spot lighting on your collections or artwork will add to the ambience and create conversation points as guests notice and start chatting about the painting that is spotlighted. I have spot lights at the top of bookshelves in my family room. Really, I turn them on only when people come over, but they do add to the feel of the room. The light catches a couple of plants on the bookcases and cascades down, illuminating little pictures on the shelves.

Nothing warms up the room like the glow of candles. Not only that, candlelight makes everyone look more beautiful, so they can't help but feel better. I scatter candles everywhere when I entertain: in the family room, dining room, around the bar, the powder room, even in the kitchen. Candles are an inexpensive way to decorate your home for a party and there are so many ways to use them. I love to scatter groups of tiny votives in cut glass holders anywhere in the house where guests will be, in little nooks, on small tabletops as well as several clusters on the buffet. I always call these holders "crystal" because they reflect the light and magnify the flame like a sparkling diamond, but since I get them at the discount store I can safely assume that they're

Be careful with scented candles. I love them and use them all over the house but never near the food. And remember that certain scents are overpowering. I try to avoid heavy florals and frilly sweet fruit scents like pear and pineapple because I find them cloying. Instead I opt for clean, crisp scents like citrus, verbena, and herbs. Also if you're using scented candles don't overdo other scented household products like plug-in air fresheners or your house will be overpoweringly scented. If you're used to lots of scent, you might not notice but your guests will.

I often shop for candles at bargain stores, if they look good and don't have dings or scratches then I'll buy them. I don't think you have to spend a lot of money on candles; in

The principal person in a picture is light. MANET

not crystal. Oh well, eye of beholder and all that. Grouping several votives in these holders is easy to do yet it looks special and casts a warm glow in any room. Or try mixing different sizes of candles, big pillar candles offset with tiny tea lights in glass holders, so you get a combination of sizes and textures. Usually when I group candles, I place them around decorative elements in a room like a little wooden box or picture frames, to highlight them with candlelight and generally add to the mix. I find this more interesting than lining up three identical candles, but it's all a matter of personal taste. I'm sure you'll agree that you just can't have too many candles!

fact this is one of those times when more is more. I'll choose to buy more cheap candles rather than fewer high-quality ones. Pillars are my preferred candles. Tapers are a bit formal, best saved for dinner tables, but pillars have a solid look. They seem somehow casual and friendly, and they come in so many different heights and widths. They're extremely practical, they don't burn much during the course of a party and so I reuse them for my next soirée. I think they look even better when they've been used for a while than when new.

One final word on candles: remember to use them only when it's dark outside—unless they're on a birthday cake.

project VELLUM-COVERED PILLAR CANDLES

This is such a great project because it transforms a plain pillar candle into something unusual or unique. What's more, this decoration does not harm the candle in anyway, so you can simply remove the vellum wrapper after the party and use the candle for your next event.

The vellum wrappers can be customized with words that suit your party's theme or style or the name of the guest of honor. You can even print a picture on the paper if you choose.

WHAT YOU'LL NEED

EQUIPMENT

- Computer and printer
- Paper cutter or scissors

MATERIALS

For each candle you will need:

- 1 sheet vellum paper
- 1 3 x 6-inch pillar candle
- Scotch tape

WHAT YOU'LL DO

1. Type your message in the computer; text should be no bigger than 3 inches wide by 4 inches tall.

2. Print out the message on vellum paper.

3. Cut vellum to size so it will wrap around the pillar candle without excess at the top, bottom, or sides.

4. Wrap (and overlap) vellum around candle and attach with Scotch tape.

5. Use any size of pillar candle that is at least 3 inches in diameter. The vellum paper text should be no longer than the diameter of the candle and at least 1 inch shorter than the candle at top and bottom.

Detail is the difference between ordinary and extraordinary.

Light Up the Night Safely

Follow the time-honored tradition of illuminating your home and creating a special party atmosphere by using candles but keep the following safety tips in mind:

- Never leave a burning candle unattended.
- Do not burn a candle if its container is cracked.
- Always place candles in hurricanes, candlesticks, votives, or other holders that will not fall over easily. Keeping candles in holders also protects surfaces as a candle can easily become hot enough to damage furniture.
- Candles must be kept out of the reach of children and pets.
- Keep candles well away from drapes, lampshades, furniture, and hanging plants—and always out of drafts.
- To avoid excessive smoking, wicks should be trimmed to ¼ inch (about the thickness of a pencil).
- Discontinue burning a candle when less than ½ inch of wax remains.
- Always make sure that candles are properly extinguished, especially before going to bed.

Glass hurricanes are the little black dress of the candle family; they look elegant with a simple off-white pillar candle inside and you can accessorize them to suit the style of your party. Another thing I adore about hurricanes is that when you dress them up for a party, you do so without damaging the candle inside, so you can use it for another event. Often I say hit the discount store, but hurricanes are one of those items that are really worth buying the best you can. Cheaper hurricanes tend to be thinner and more fragile than the better-quality ones. Thick glass hurricanes are a proper investment for your entertaining arsenal. There are hurricanes in all sorts of sizes in my arsenal and I use them endlessly. After so many parties, some are a little chipped on the edge but no one can tell.

INTO THE GROOVE

Music is a powerful mood maker; no celebration is complete without it. Arriving at a party where the room is decorated and the food set out, if there's no music playing in the background you feel you're too early—the party isn't swinging because no tunes are playing. Music does more than alleviate any painful silences; it can invigorate, relax, or inspire dancing on the rug. As DJ, one of your duties is to keep the music going throughout the night—without interruption. Either program several CDs into your disc changer, attach an iPod, or create some mixed CDs for your party.

I always choose my tunes carefully. Usually I go with something subtle, instrumentals like classical cello and Spanish flamenco or low-key vocals like Sarah McLachlan, Dido, and Sting. Cocktails need something more upbeat I think, so then I opt for swing or standards. And for a theme party, I go all out with the music. At Halloween I figure it's a cheesy party so I play cheesy '80s music, anything from Journey to Depeche Mode. A barbecue on the patio with big

drinks might inspire a Jimmy Buffet soundtrack but I'd never play that indoors! And when I cook a certain cuisine I try to play music from the same country: with French bistro-type food I'd play Les Négresses Vertes or Les Nubians or maybe a movie soundtrack like *Amélie*. It's a great way to learn about other cultures and introduce your friends and yourself to new music. If you don't have time to dig through your CD collection, try one of the mixed CDs made for a certain mood—you'll find them on sale everywhere from gourmet cookware stores to discounters.

The first CD of the night is the most important; it's playing when there are only a few people around and is really "instrumental" in getting the party into the right gear, so decide what you'll play first. Whatever music you choose, be sure to try it out on your CD player. Check what volume is high enough so everyone can hear it but low enough that they can still hear each other talk, so you can set the volume just right on the night.

DRESSING UP THE ATMOSPHERE

The first step to creating atmosphere is defining what kind of mood you'd like your party to have. That wasn't hard for the Little Black Dress Dinner Party; fancy and formal but not stuffy has been my guiding principle ever since I first cooked up the idea for this party. It's going to be a dress-up affair and needs to feel really special.

The lighting won't be that different from the usual, the lights will be dimmed, and I'll use my favorite cream pillar candles in hurricanes around the family room, the foyer, even in the kitchen on the breakfast bar, and on the dinner table. I'm not going to use any flowers. I could have some little arrangements in the family room and to pretty up the breakfast bar hors d'oeuvres spread or I could make a floral cen-terpiece but I don't think I will. I'd like to do something out of the ordinary, something more unexpected for this dinner party. Flowers are always appropriate and I love them but this time I'm going to do something different.

The music should be low key; perhaps I'll play that classical CD of *Bach Cello Suites* by Ros-tropovich. It's not that I'm a classical buff, nor are our guests, but it's lovely and really sets a tony yet friendly mood. I never play vocal music during a dinner party because I think the singing competes too much with the dinner table conversation. I might pop on some Harry Connick Jr. or even some Frank (Sinatra) if we move to the family room after dessert is finished.

BLOOMING LOVELY

Flowers add freshness and life to any room. You might want to use flowers on the table or as decorations in the party room; even if you aren't having a floral centerpiece you can still use flowers elsewhere to brighten the scene. However, watch your wallet when buying flowers. It's easy to get caught up in the beauty of the blooms and spend much more than you can afford. The best way to avoid this is to budget how much you can spend and spend only that much or less, no more. And before you shop have a clear idea of what you want to buy and in what colors; think about what suits the style of your party, relaxed flowers in a simple container for a casual party, a more exuberant and formal arrangement in a crystal or porcelain vase for a more dressed up event. A wedding shower should be light and cheerful so maybe daisies would be the thing. You can have fun with flowers too; I use black-red roses for my Halloween party. For an English-style afternoon tea I'd fill a low silver container with soft pink flowers.

Work out how many vases of flowers you want to have so you can calculate how many flowers you need to buy. Consider containers; be sure you have suitable vases or other containers for the flowers you plan to buy. I use all kinds of containers, everything from interesting tins to big pitchers and jars to wooden boxes. Often I line the container with a glass

jar or vase and put the water and flowers in that, not into the container directly. And always shop with some back-up options in case your first-choice flower is not available or is too pricey. If you're lucky enough to have backyard blooms, give them a starring role in your party décor.

If fresh flowers are too expensive or just don't suit your party, try going green. Potted plants with interesting foliage such as boxwoods are great; you can trim them into a shape if you like. I also like unusual ivies; buy them in tiny plastic pots for next to nothing and repot them into a container that works better with the look of your party. Another option is to use flowering potted plants. I adore hydrangeas. I put them in decorative pots and have them around the house, not just when I'm entertaining but I'll rope them in and use them for an event if they look right for the party. Potted bulbs, anything from paperwhites to tulips or amaryllis, don't cost much, look great, and you can enjoy them beyond your party, perhaps even plant them in the backyard for next year.

Keep 'Em Fresh:
Follow These Tips to Keep Flowers Looking Their Best

- If cutting your own blooms, cut flowers in the early morning or late evening and immediately place in cool, fresh water.
- For bought flowers, immediately upon returning home, cut ends of stems on the diagonal and remove any leaves or offshoots that will remain below the waterline—submerged foliage can rot and encourage bacteria which shortens the life span of the flowers. Then place in cool, fresh water.
- It usually takes a day or so for blooms to fully open up. For best results, arrange your flowers the day before your party so the flowers have a chance to be their fullest (this also saves you more time on the day of the party). Roses can be particularly slow to open and sometimes may take two days to really open up.
- When ready to arrange flowers for the party, fill the vase or container about halfway with fresh, cool water, then add cut-flower food. Hold each stem next to the vase to gauge how much you'll need to trim. Using a very sharp knife or floral shears, cut the stem ends underwater at a 45-degree angle to encourage water absorption. Arrange flowers in the vase as desired.
- Flowers are best kept in a cool room away from drafts. Also keep them away from direct sunlight as it will speed the wilting process.
- Some flowers need reconditioning daily, others require care every two to three days. Ask the florist how often the flowers you choose will need refreshing. To recondition flowers: cut the stems, change the water, and add cut-flower food, or a tablespoon of sugar, and two drops of liquid bleach to the water.

FLOWERS SEASON BY SEASON

WHAT'S AVAILABLE WHEN

Spring

Anemones
Apple blossoms
Cherry blossoms
Daffodils
Dogwoods
Forsythia branches
Freesia
Hyacinth
Iris
Larkspur
Lilacs
Lilies
Lily of the Valley
Magnolia
Pansies
Peonies
Sweet Peas
Tulips
Violets

Summer

Asters
Bells of Ireland
Calla Lilies
Dahlias
Delphinium
Forget-me-nots
Fuschia
Geraniums
Gladiola
Honeysuckle
Hydrangeas
Iris
Jacob's Ladder
Larkspur
Shasta daisies
Stock
Sunflower
Sweet William
Zinnias
Goldenrod

Fall

Asters
Chinese lanterns
Chrysanthemums
Dahlia
Dried hydrangeas
Gerbera daisies
Marigolds
Zinnias

Foliage

Autumn leaves
Rosehip
Rosemary
Yarrow

Winter

Amaryllis
Camellias
Hyacinths
Paperwhite narcissus
Poinsettias
Tulips

Foliage

Fern
Ivy
Pine
Rhododendron leaves
Spruce

Year around

Carnations
Daisies
Ferns
Gardenias
Ivy
Lilies
Orchids
Roses
Tulips
Snapdragons
Stephanotis

THEMED DECORATIONS

For a theme party, whether it's a Halloween bash, a birthday celebration, or a baby shower, I always like to make some special decorations that reflect the theme of the event. If there's no time or you don't feel crafty, hit the party supply store to see if it has something you can use or embellish for party decorations. Decorations don't have to be confined to the main party room. Try putting something on the porch or in the foyer where everyone will see it as they arrive; it will help get them in the mood for the party.

As I enjoy making decorations, I often make signs and arrangements for birthdays or showers or seek out things that I can use to add to a theme, like old movie reels from a secondhand store. A stack made perfect décor for an Oscar party—plus I covered some with glass and used them as hors d'oeuvre platters. So get thinking, have fun with the theme. Themed decorations add to the party spirit and can be fun icebreakers for guests.

project HANDMADE LETTERED SIGN ("IT'S A GIRL")

This technique for making a lettered sign is not only for baby showers; use it to make a big Happy Birthday sign, Congratulations, Merry Christmas, or any other message you might want your guests to read in readiness for the party ahead. Pin it on the door, the wall, or across the front of the buffet table.

WHAT YOU'LL NEED

EQUIPMENT
• Scissors

MATERIALS
• *I, T, S, A, G, R, L* attachable letters from party
  store (buy two of each letter needed)
• 4 sheets 8½ x 11 colored card stock

• 4 sheets 8½ x 11 card stock in a coordinating color
• Spray adhesive
• Small paper flowers (optional)
• Glue gun and glue sticks, or liquid glue (optional)
• Scotch tape
• Fishing line

WHAT YOU'LL DO

1. Cut tabs off letters.

2. Cut the beveled ¼-inch edge off one of each type of letter (one *I,* one *G,* etc.).

3. Then using the letters that still have the beveled edge, trace each letter on one color of card stock. (Be sure to trace the *I* twice.) There should be room for two letters per sheet of card stock.

4. Trace smaller unbeveled letters on the other card stock. (Be sure to trace the *I* twice.)

5. Using spray adhesive, attach each smaller cut letter to the front of the corresponding larger letter.

6. If desired, use glue to attach small paper flowers, evenly spaced on the centers of each letter.

7. Place the letters face down on the floor spacing them how you want them spaced.

8. Tape fishing line across the back of the letters, placing the fishing line about 1 inch from the top toward the top of each letter.

Journal Entry

Make a quick plan of what lighting you'll be using for the party. Also note how many candles you need to buy, where you intend to put them, and if you need them, what decorations to buy for the hurricanes.

Make a music list of what CDs you've selected for the party and what you've chosen to play first.

Keep info on ideas for flowers and the price and sources plus what vases or containers you'll be using. If you're using themed decorations, make a list of what to buy or the supplies for making them, and note where you'll be putting them for the party.

CHAPTER 10

THE *Table*

My mother and father always entertained a lot—they still do—so our fine china didn't stay in dusty closets or come out only at Thanksgiving; we ate off it at least once a week. My mom kept her dishes in a huge buffet where everything was arranged by pattern. When she'd let me choose the china for a dinner party I'd always select the pattern with tiny hand-painted flowers. I loved those plates and would run my fingers lightly over the flowers to feel the bumps, pausing to admire the brightly painted flowers. My mom knew how to set a table and, in addition to arranging the china, would also add handwritten place cards and individual salt and pepper shakers to each setting. Those little details were my very favorite things back then. (This was long before Martha. . . .) They still are.

Just as an invitation sets the tone for the party and creates excitement and anticipation for what's to come, the
table sets the tone for the meal. Setting the table is like
dressing the stage for the show, the main event—the

food. Doesn't food seem to taste better when served in
pleasant surroundings? I believe so. And I also believe
that food is not only a matter of taste—first we eat with
our eyes.

It is around the table that friends understand best

ON THE TABLE

For me, setting a table is a three-step program. Sometimes the table might need only the one-step approach,
other occasions two is just right. I have to admit, though,
I do love it when I get the opportunity to do all three:

1. Details of necessity—plates, flatware, stemware,
napkins

2. Details of decadence—linens, candles, centerpieces

3. Details of fun—place cards, menus, teeny table
presents (favors), individual salt and pepper shakers, cards or books of toasts

DETAILS OF NECESSITY

These are the things you *need* to entertain: plates, flatware, stemware, and napkins. They are the foundation
pieces of your entertaining arsenal and once you have them
you can set a simply stylish table. You can dress down or
jazz up these necessities by adding different colors, patterns, or textures to the mix, layering and using items in unexpected ways to create many different table looks. When
mixing, make sure there is at least one common element

among the pieces that will hold the look together. Mixing
does not mean haphazardly throwing different things on the
table, but rather using pieces with coordinating colors and
textures, a similar proportion, or complementary styles to
make the table harmonious. Basic arsenal pieces can be
used for any occasion. You don't need china or crystal to
entertain or even to host a formal dinner.

The way your food is presented has a lot to do with the table it rests on. Think about an entrée at a fancy restaurant. If you were served the same food on a paper plate in a fast-food restaurant would it taste as good? Probably not. Maybe that explains how a high-end restaurant in Atlanta can charge $26 for a hamburger! It's served on fine china with linen napkins.

the warmth of being together. DENISE ROBIN

project STAMPED PLATE

I always use real plates when I have guests over. They're so much nicer than paper. Instead of using paper plates at your next event, try embellishing inexpensive plain white ceramic plates with stamps. The plates I used were only fifty cents each, roughly the same as decorator paper plates. Any plain glazed ceramic, china, or glass plate will work. Choose a rubber stamp with a bold design as any fine detail will not reproduce as well on the plate. This technique is great for parties—you can change the look of the plates for each party for next to nothing. And if you don't like the look of the plate after stamping or it doesn't come out right the first time, you can just rinse the plate and try again. When using edible inks, you can stamp the design anywhere on the plate, on the rim or in center where it will be in contact with food, but note that if the edible inks come into contact with food they will run so plates stamped with gel food coloring are best used for drier foods. And when using gel food coloring, the stamp pad must be prepared the night before you stamp the plates.

WHAT YOU'LL NEED

MATERIALS
- Plain cocktail or dessert plate, washed and dried
- Clean wood-mounted rubber stamp
- Un-inked sponge stamp pad
- Gel food coloring
- Stamp cleaner
- Paper towel

WHAT YOU'LL DO

1. Use the gel food coloring to saturate the sponge ink pad. Leave the top off the pad overnight to allow the ink to become somewhat tacky.

2. Place the plate on a flat surface. Turn the rubber stamp onto its wood side with the rubber facing up, take the opened stamp pad and lightly tap the rubber side of the stamp, covering it completely with ink. Be careful not to over-ink your stamp.

3. Using a straight up and down motion, place the rubber stamp on plate exactly where you want image to be. Once stamp touches the plate, do not shift or rock it from side to side or image will be distorted. Apply even pressure on back of stamp by running the pads of your fingers all over the surface area of the wood backing. Lift the stamp straight up to remove.

4. Allow to dry, preferably overnight. When party is over, wash plates as normal; stamped images will disappear.

5. When finished with stamping, use stamp cleaner and paper towels to clean the rubber stamp. (Do not rinse rubber stamps under running water because the excess water will break down the glue holding the rubber stamp to the wood block.)

VARIATION WITH SEMIPERMANENT INK

Substitute solid-surface, permanent water-based ink pad for the gel food coloring and un-inked stamp pad. Stamp plate on rim only; do no not stamp in center/food contact area.

Note: Using this ink, the image will wash off after a couple of washes or can be removed by scrubbing with a dishwashing brush and soap.

Take a Seat

Take some time to consider your seating arrangements. If you aren't using place cards, be prepared to direct your guests to their seats or assign your partner to this traffic directing task. And as for the etiquette of who should sit where, well, as hostess you should sit at the head of the table. The table has two heads so you get to choose which you want. Best to select the most convenient seat for kitchen access. Your partner should claim the other. (If your table is round, it still has a head, and that's wherever you sit.)

A guest of honor should be placed to your right. If you're honoring two guests, seat one to your right and the other to your partner's right. Or, if you think your guests of honor would rather be closer, seat them opposite each other, one to your right and the other to your left.

I find that people talk most to the person opposite them, so I generally seat couples next to each other. That way they can play footsie if they want, but can also engage in conversation with the person across the table. If it's a mixed group, I do the old boy-girl-boy-girl thing. And if some of the guests don't know each other, I'll take care to seat them so they will be pulled into conversation, beside a chatty friend, perhaps, or maybe next to me.

DETAILS OF DECADENCE

Once you go beyond the necessities you reach a certain level of decadence. The table becomes a canvas for expressing your personal style. The details of decadence—linens, candles, centerpieces—add texture, light, color, and visual appeal to the table. No one needs a table runner, but it can be a lovely decorative touch. A bold colored runner on a plain table gives it a more dressy look. Less formal than a tablecloth, a runner can be particularly effective when used with a centerpiece that echoes its long shape. I know you can eat at a plain wooden table but somehow it just seems more polished with a cloth on the table; it's that $26 hamburger scenario. To me a tablecloth is the base on which you set everything, the backdrop that pulls everything together. If you're buying a tablecloth, consider it an investment for your entertaining arsenal. I suggest something in cream or taupe so it's a neutral background for the table. Then put your personality into the table setting with other details, the centerpiece or the fun elements to come.

project BASIC HEMMED TABLECLOTH

Change the look of your table completely—and add to your arsenal supplies—by making a simple sewn tablecloth. You don't even need a sewing machine to make this cloth if you use Stitch Witchery, a fusible hem tape. Many different types of fabric are suitable for this project; just make sure the one you choose is washable. I like to use cotton decorator fabrics which are easy to work with and easy to maintain.

WHAT YOU'LL NEED

EQUIPMENT

- Iron
- Sewing machine or Stitch Witchery
- Scissors
- Measuring tape

MATERIALS

- 1 piece fabric, 2 feet longer and 2 feet wider than your table
- Coordinating thread

WHAT YOU'LL DO

FOR SEWING MACHINE:

1. Fold over each edge $3/8$ inches and press.

2. Fold each fold over again $3/8$ inches and press.

3. Stitch folded hems on sewing machine.

VARIATION USING STITCH WITCHERY

1. Fold over each edge $3/8$ inches and press.

2. Fold each fold over again $3/8$ inches and press.

3. Open second fold and insert Stitch Witchery underneath.

4. Place fold back down and press with an iron on hot setting.

A table cloth is the base on which
you set everything,
the backdrop that pulls everything together.

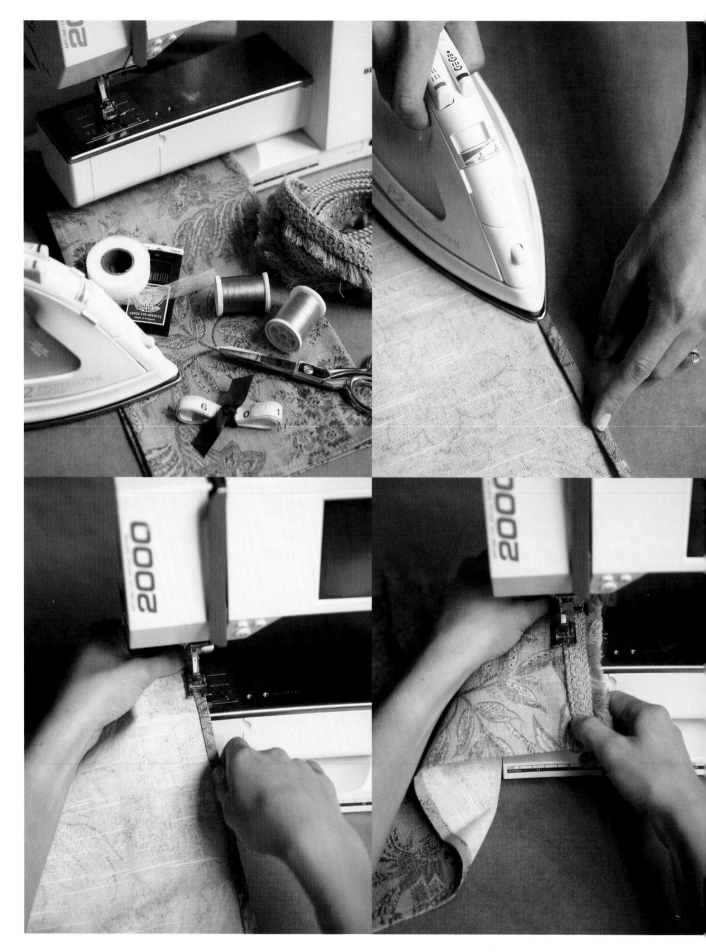

project NAPKINS WITH WISPY FRINGE

Use a washable fabric to make these fanciful napkins. Just as for the tablecloth, if you don't have a sewing machine, you can make them using Stitch Witchery. The instructions below are for one napkin and can be scaled up accordingly; I made them for a dinner for six.

WHAT YOU'LL NEED

EQUIPMENT

- Iron
- Sewing machine or Stitch Witchery
- Scissors
- Measuring tape

MATERIALS

- $17\frac{1}{2}$-inch-square piece of fabric for each napkin
- Coordinating thread
- 1 yard decorative trim

WHAT YOU'LL DO

FOR SEWING MACHINE:

1. Fold over each edge $\frac{3}{8}$ inch and press.

2. Fold each fold over again $\frac{3}{8}$ inch and press.

3. Stitch folded hems on sewing machine.

4. Pin and stitch decorative trim around at least two adjoining sides on sewing machine, or add trim to all four edges if desired.

VARIATION USING STITCH WITCHERY

1. Fold over each edge $\frac{3}{8}$ inch and press.

2. Fold each fold over again $\frac{3}{8}$ inch and press.

3. Open second fold and insert Stitch Witchery underneath.

4. Place fold back down and press with an iron on hot setting.

5. Place Stitch Witchery below trim on edges of napkin and iron on high heat until trim is attached.

Note: You may need to iron longer so the heat can reach adhesive through the thicker trim piece.

project STRING OF PEARLS NAPKIN RING

Pearls make a lovely dressy napkin ring. Substitute chunky wooden beads and you'd get a very different mood. In fact there are as many possible looks with this project as there are types of beads in the craft store. Use buttons to create a funky napkin ring or try those tiny Christmas bells for a truly seasonal napkin holder.

WHAT YOU'LL NEED

EQUIPMENT

• Scissors

MATERIALS

For each napkin ring:

• One 9-inch piece of Stretch Magic bead and jewelry cord

• 10 large pearl beads

• 4 silver and crystal 6 mm rondels (spacers)

WHAT YOU'LL DO

1. Tie a double knot at one end of the jewelry cord.

2. Thread three pearl beads onto cord. Thread one spacer onto cord.

3. Thread two pearl beads onto cord. Thread one spacer onto cord.

4. Repeat step 2. Knot cord three times and cut off excess cord.

When I invite people over I like to have a focal point on the table. A centerpiece is basically just a dressing for the table; it has no other function than to be pretty. There are certain rules to obey when creating a centerpiece; it should be below eye level so guests can see the person opposite and not too wide or sprawling so that it creeps into the place settings.

If you say "centerpiece" to most people they'll picture a flower arrangement. You can make an arrangement for the center of the table—the only limit is your imagination—but a centerpiece does not have to contain flowers. Any decorative item that fills the dead space in the center of the table can serve as a centerpiece. At its most basic, a pillar candle in a plain hurricane set in the middle of the table is a centerpiece. Whether pillars in hurricanes, tapers in a formal candlestick, or votives in those cut-glass holders I like so much, candles add atmosphere to the table either alone or combined with flowers, greenery, or other things. Be careful with candles when used together with other elements, particularly dry materials or artificial greenery—the heat from the flame travels beyond the actual flame, and never set a candle directly on the table as wax or heat may damage the surface. So always set candles in holders or on a small dish or coaster.

When working with flowers as a centerpiece, remember to keep the arrangement low and don't use very fragrant blooms such as paperwhites. Think of other natural elements that would make centerpieces suited to the style of your party: a branch with pine cones; a pyramid of oranges or lemons atop a cake stand; a giant conch shell illuminated by votives. Or other simple items that deserve the spotlight. If you have a glass bowl filled with colored marbles use it. Create your centerpieces with a sense of humor, adventure, or wonder; anything can be a centerpiece as long as it's low and pretty.

GREENERY CENTERPIECE

Something you already have on display in your home, such as a flowering plant in a pretty pot or a collection of ferns in a trough can be moved to the table to make an interesting centerpiece.

project ROSE GIFT BOX

I like flower balls but felt I'd seen them one too many times—so I made a box instead. When I'd done it I was so pleased, I realized the box was just the thing to flag the gift table at the baby shower I was planning—oh, and it makes a lovely centerpiece too.

The Rose Gift Box I made was really special and over the top. You can make a smaller one with fewer bricks of florist's foam and fewer flowers. Use flowers all of one color or use a different shade for the top few rows to give the illusion of a box lid.

Try covering this box with carnations, mums, or any relatively compact and sturdy flower. I use double-faced ribbon in most of my projects so that there is no "wrong" side of the ribbon to show such as for the bow on this box. I often choose wired ribbon because I find it easier to tie a beautiful bow with it; tweaking the wires lets me keep the bow full and fluffed up.

WHAT YOU'LL NEED

EQUIPMENT

- Scissors
- Pruners or floral knife

MATERIALS

- 6 or 8 bricks Oasis
- Floral tape
- About 5 dozen roses
- 4 yards 1½ x 2-inch-wide ribbon

WHAT YOU'LL DO

1. Stack three floral foam bricks. Tape them together with floral tape. Repeat with remaining three bricks.

2. Tape the two stacks together to create a large cube.

3. Soak Oasis in water until moist, about 15–20 minutes.

4. Use floral knife to trim stems of roses to about 4 inches.

Insert roses into foam in rows, filling all surfaces of the foam. On two uppermost rows of flowers, let roses stick out about ½ inch more than the rest of the cube to give the illusion of a box lid.

5. Once cube is completely covered in roses, tie "gift box" with ribbon as if wrapping a present. Finish with a large bow on the top.

DETAILS OF FUN

Why bother? Place cards, menus, teeny table presents (favors), individual salt and pepper shakers, cards, or books of toasts are unexpected, unnecessary even, but they are appreciated by guests and often spark conversation.

Actually place cards are useful; they give everyone direction on where to sit and avoid that awkward moment when two people go for the same chair—no you take it, no you—or when people are wondering if they should take a seat or if someone else will want that seat and be miffed if they take it. Giving everyone seat assignments means you get them seated faster. I've heard that people sometimes want to change their seat; luckily it's never happened to me—yet! If it did, I'd put my gracious hostess hat on and go with the flow, still feeling amazed at the cheek of them asking!

Menu cards are kind of useful too. They let your guests know what is to come, and above all, they create excitement. When guests see their own individual menu at their place, they feel fancy. The menu cards bring an element of formality to the table yet they don't cost much to make and the longest part of making them is formatting the text on the computer. It takes so little extra time to make six or eight menu cards that I always make one for each dinner guest rather than one or two for the table.

BIRDCAGE CENTERPIECE

Sometimes it is fun to go all out and create a centerpiece
that really matches the décor of your party. This whimsical creation, though reminiscent of something you'd see
in an eighteenth-century still-life painting, was made
with finds from my discount and dollar-store trips.

MENU

First Course
Cranberry Blue Cheese Tartlet
and Mixed Greens with a Mustard Vinaigrette

Second Course
Herbed Rack of Lamb
with a Red Wine Reduction

Spring Vegetables and
Baby Potatoes

Dessert
Mini Chocolate Molten Cakes
with Whipped Cream

project PRINTED MENU

A menu card is useful and lovely and can become a memento of the evening. I've had guests want to take the menu card home with them, so sometimes I add other details about the party, the place, date, guests, or a quote at the bottom of the menu listings.

There are many ways to dress up the menu card. One of my favorites is to punch two holes at the top of the card and thread ribbon through them, tying a big bow. Often I'll add a charm or bead or button to further embellish it.

WHAT YOU'LL NEED

EQUIPMENT

- Computer and printer
- Paper cutter or scissors
- Hole punch (optional)

MATERIALS

For each menu card:

- 2 sheets coordinating paper, one sheet must be printer friendly
- 1 sheet card stock or heavyweight paper
- Spray mount adhesive or double-stick tape
- Ribbon, $1/4$ to $1 1/2$ inches wide, can be wired or un-wired (optional)

WHAT YOU'LL DO

1. Choose a font that goes with the theme or look of the party. Type the menu, leave spaces between each course, and center the text on the page. Print a sample on a sheet of plain paper. Make any changes necessary, then once the wording is correct, print using the printer-friendly paper.

2. Use a paper cutter to cut the card stock to 5 x 7 inches. Cut the coordinating paper so it is slightly smaller than the card stock, approximately $4 3/4$ x $6 3/4$ inches. Trim the printed page so it is slightly smaller than the coordinating paper, about $4 1/2$ x $6 1/2$ inches.

3. Use spray mount adhesive to attach the printed menu to the paper, then attach the paper to the card stock.

4. Punch holes, $3/4$ inch apart, in top of menu card. Thread ribbon through holes and tie a bow on front of card (optional).

A FEW OF MY FAVORITE THINGS

Individual salt and pepper shakers make guests oooh and aaah. They're tiny and not super-practical, but there's just something about getting your very own set that makes people happy. If you're an avid flea marketer you'll likely be able to pick up unusual vintage shakers on your antiquing trips; otherwise check the shelves at the discount store—that's where I found mine.

Teeny table presents are pretty similar to favors but in order for something to work as a table favor, it really does have to be small. I've given wrapped gifts on the table before; one I especially liked was tiny ring-sized boxes wrapped in luxe paper at a holiday dinner party. Inside each was a mini-ornament. More fun and more unexpected are quotes or toasts, written on a piece of paper or card stock and hidden under the dinner plates. They are revealed when you remove the plates to take them to plate the entrée. While you're busy in the kitchen, everyone is amused by reading and sharing the quotes or toasts they've discovered at their place. You can go one step further and buy teeny tiny two-inch square toast or quote books, or go six steps further and create your own minibook either on the computer or by hand. Fill it with favorite quotes, quotes on a certain theme, or even with what my friend Dawn labeled "after-party quotes." She compiled a minibook of what she calls "the things you might think during a party but know better than to say out loud." They're hilarious.

ALL THE DETAILS

The look of the room and the table is often the first thing I imagine when I plan a party. The colors I picture may well inspire or inform the menu and the rest of the party. It was a bit different for the Little Black Dress Dinner. It was going to be a special dinner party for Todd but I didn't really have a look in mind until I started to play with that Little Black Dress idea. I thought of my basic entertaining arsenal being like the little black dress of entertaining equipment; you can play it up or dress it down, accessorize those cream plates in so many different ways. So then I thought this was an occasion to play dress up with the basic arsenal equipment, and what is more classy than a string of pearls with a little black dress? That's where the inspiration for the napkin ring came from!

As I've used these basic plates so many times for more casual meals, I wanted to make them seem different—that's where all the details of decadence and fun come in. Though it looks properly formal, remember no fancy china or crystal was used in the making of this tablescape. I'm really happy with it; this classic tone-on-tone look is never out of style. It's truly timeless and seems just right for a grown-up dinner party where guests will wear their party frocks and jewels.

As you have learned, I *love* candles and thought I'd really play them up on this table. Not the candles themselves as much as that lovely glow they create, which I'm hoping will play up the pearly, lustrous look of the table.

project BUFFET DISH CARDS

Essential for a buffet or even a cocktail party spread, these cards explain what a dish is and note any main ingredients that a guest may be allergic to. You could also use them to identify cheeses at a wine and cheese tasting. A versatile project, this basic computer and card-stock technique can also be used to make card-stock place cards for a seated event.

WHAT YOU'LL NEED

EQUIPMENT

- Computer and printer
- Paper cutter or scissors

MATERIALS

For each menu or place card you will need:

- 1 sheet card stock cut to $3\frac{1}{2}$ inches wide by 3 inches high
- 1 sheet coordinating printer-friendly paper or card stock cut to $3\frac{1}{4}$ inches wide by $2\frac{3}{4}$ inches high
- 1 sheet coordinating paper
- Spray adhesive

WHAT YOU'LL DO

1. Select a font that suits the style of the party. Type name and main ingredients of each dish or, if making place cards, type each person's name into your computer. Make the words as large as possible for it to fit in a 3 x $2\frac{1}{2}$-inch rectangle. Print a sample on plain paper and check that spellings are correct and there are no typos. Then print on sheet of coordinating printer-friendly paper.

2. Cut the printed paper to 3 inches wide by $2\frac{1}{2}$ inches high. Use spray mount adhesive to attach it to the coordinating paper or card stock. Then attach the papers to card stock. Place finished buffet menu cards in place-card holder or mini-easel for display on buffet or table.

A self-service spread seems informal but that doesn't mean you should skip the tabletop décor. You can incorporate all the same elements of necessity, decadence, and fun that you would for a sit-down meal. Think of setting a buffet as a progression; set it in the order that things will be used. Place plates at one end of the table and utensils and napkins at the other. This lets guests serve themselves without juggling knives, forks, and napkins. If a food is served with rice, place the rice first so guests can set the food on top of the rice, and if there is a sauce, put it on the other side of the food.

With its abundance of food, a buffet is a decoration in itself. Make the most of the display by playing with shapes, sizes, and colors of platters; use table linens with patterns or textures; or place a runner or a topper over the tablecloth. The buffet should have up-and-down motion as you cast your eye across it, so serve some food in footed serving dishes, some in low platters, some in bowls or on pedestal cake stands.

Journal Entry

Go through your entertaining arsenal and check that the pieces you will be using are in good shape. Make a list of what you'll be using from the arsenal plus a list of any tabletop items you need to buy. Note ideas for a centerpiece and any other projects you'll be making plus what materials you need to purchase for them.

Sketch a plan of how the table or buffet will look. Also draw a seating plan of who will be where.

Check and polish silverware well before the day of the party—two weeks or ten days before is fine.

CHAPTER 11

Playing Favorites
. . . AND FAVORS

How's this for romance: a long time ago (some might say "in days of yore . . .") a lady would give a favor, such as an embroidered hand-kerchief, a glove, or lock of hair to a knight she loved or admired. That tradition has evolved somewhat from its lovelorn origins. Today, while a favor can still be a token of love, it's usually regarded as a small gift given out at a party—think children's goody bags, for example, or those bags of sugared almonds distributed to guests at weddings and baby showers. Favors are not essential to entertaining. No one's going to think any less of you for sending your guests home without a keepsake, especially after you have graciously invited them to your place for the evening. Yet there's just something about favors; they round out the evening so nicely and can be such a fun way to thank guests for coming to your home. And they can really end the evening on a high note. It's the last thing guests will see, a keepsake to take home and a reminder of you and your spectacular soirée.

A favor should be inexpensive, generally no more than $5 to $10 each. And while it doesn't have to be small in size, somehow I always seem to end up giving special *little* things. Making favors is truly a time when less is more, so think of something creative to match the theme or style of your party, and of course your personal style. Favors can be as simple or elaborate as you like. They can be made from scratch, store-bought, or a combination of both.

Whether you choose to make, buy, or embellish, the key to great favors is imagination, careful shopping, and clever presentation. I'm a bargain shopper and love to go through dollar stores and discount retailers in search of cheap fun things. I keep my eye open for potential favors even when

ded paper at the bottom, and a wide, wired, satin ribbon in a bright plaid that echoed the colors of the gels and lotions, these dollar bottles took on the look of froufrou bath-shop items. For my happy hour wine party I paired an inexpensive but useful old-school wood-handled corkscrew with discount store cocktail napkins that were so cute I couldn't resist them. All I did was tie them together with raffia. After a dinner party where I served Chinese food, everyone went home with fortune cookies in a pretty patterned takeout food box. Clever or beautiful wrapping can elevate dollar store purchases—sometimes it really is all in the wrapping.

No act of kindness, no matter how small, is ever wasted. AESOP

I'm not planning a party. The top-quality miniature footballs I got for a dollar each on clearance reappeared months later as favors for a Super Bowl party. Everyone loved them and no one knew I'd bought them on sale. (Until now, that is.)

If you are pressed for time but still want to give favors, then buying something and wrapping it beautifully is the way to go. When my girlfriends came for a slumber party I played up the hotel sleepover theme by giving them favors of bath gels and lotions in the same minisizes you get in hotels. Packed in cellophane bags, with bright pink shred-

Store-bought Favors

- Champagne splits wrapped with a colorful ribbon.
- Bars of high-quality chocolate, such as Godiva or Ghirardelli, which you can personalize by making a new label to put over the bar's original wrapping. You could print details of the occasion (when and what it was for) and also include a little *thanks for coming* note. Or you could buy a large size of individually wrapped chocolate squares and pack them in cellophane bags tied with ribbon to coordinate with the wrapping on the chocolate.
- Small potted herb plants tied with a simple recipe that uses the herb—pesto, pasta sauce with fresh oregano.
- Small bag of coffee with an individualized label. (A friend of mine gave these out at a wedding shower. The groom's name was Joseph, so the label read *"Not your average Joe!"*)
- Movie rental gift cards plus microwave popcorn and a box or two of "movie-size" candy packed into a popcorn bucket.
- Wax seals with recipient's initial and wax.
- Little photo albums with recipes, quotes, or pictures inside.
- Picture books and bookmarks (check out the clearance aisle at your local bookstore).
- Miniature (airline-size) bottles of the liquor used for the party's signature drink with the drink recipe.
- Drug store manicure kits with latest polish color.
- Note cards with recipients' initials.
- Bath gel, bath salts, or something that smells good for the bath and a natural sponge tied together with ribbon.
- Ready-made CDs with the music from the party; for example, if you played standards at the party, give CDs of standards bought on clearance.
- Gourmet BBQ sauces or rubs: something from an unusual local store, or a gourmet brand from Williams-Sonoma.
- Holiday-specific items such as ornaments at Christmas or seasoned mini-wreaths for Thanksgiving.

When you have more time and feel like warming up the glue gun, embellish a store-bought object. This can be as straightforward as hot-gluing ribbon decorations onto inexpensive slippers and tying them with more ribbon; I did that for favors for a lazy Sunday girls hangout party. Sometimes you can transform a store-bought item so no one would guess its humble origins, like the supersized container of discount store bath milk I used to fill baby bottles for the Southern Afternoon Tea Baby Shower favor.

project DELUXE PARTY MUSIC CD

Making a party favor CD of the music played at the event is a truly fun project. Not only do you get to organize the music for the party, but you get to make the favor at the same time. I've usually made a CD favor for bigger parties, like my annual Halloween bash or when I've hosted a party with a theme so that the music has a common thread. Guests who would never buy an opera CD will get an intro-

duction to this music and maybe even become fans. One of my favorite CDs was made by my friend Dawn for a BBQ party she hosted. It's all country music and she called it "All That and a Bottle of Beer."

I like to make a card-stock envelope for CDs; it's less expensive and more of an expression of my style than using a jewel case. For a simpler project, decorate a jewel case for the CD.

WHAT YOU'LL NEED FOR THE CD AND ENVELOPE

EQUIPMENT

- Computer and printer
- Scissors
- Paper cutter

MATERIALS

- Collection of songs that will be played at your event
- 1 blank CD
- 1 CD label

- 1 sheet heavyweight card stock
- Permanent double-stick tape
- 1 piece sticker paper: Avery full sheet label printer paper
- 1 sheet decorative or colored paper (any weight)
- Spray mount adhesive
- 11 inches coordinating 1-inch-wide double-faced satin or grosgrain ribbon

WHAT YOU'LL DO

1. From a website that sells music, select twelve songs that will play during your party. Just be careful as there are potential legal issues with downloading music. Many services offer different options to do this legally, so be sure to check them out.

2. Create a CD label according to label manufacturer's directions and/or software.

3. For the CD envelope: trace the template (see Resources, page 243) and copy onto the card stock. Cut template from card stock. Fold card stock in half and fold tabs down so they touch the half of the rectangle without tabs. Place a strip of permanent double-stick tape along the tabs. Create a pocket by pressing tabs to the tab-less back square of the card stock.

4. Type the information that will appear on the front of the CD envelope—such as the occasion and date of the event and a title if you want to name the CD—on your computer. Center text on the page. Then, in the same document, type the names of the songs and artists on the back of the CD envelope and center text. Make sure front text area does not exceed 3 inches square; the smaller the better. The back text area should not exceed 4 inches overall. Separate the front title and CD information text areas on the page—when this information is printed both pieces of text should be centered so that you can cut the two squares for each CD from each printed sheet.

5. (Optional) Place a decorative box or border around each of the two text areas. Print a copy on plain paper to make sure information and size is correct, then print on sticker sheet.

6. Use paper cutter or scissors to cut text areas to size. Then cut two $4\frac{1}{2}$-inch-square pieces from decorative paper. Use spray mount adhesive or double-stick tape to attach the $4\frac{1}{2}$-inch squares to the center squares of the card-stock pocket, one on the front and one on the back.

7. Holding the pocket with the opening at top, wrap the ribbon horizontally, centering it around the pocket with the raw ends meeting on the back. Secure ribbon ends together with double-stick tape.

8. Attach printed label to front, centering it with the pocket square, with ribbon running underneath the label. Press down evenly on label. Attach printed label to back, centering it with the pocket square, with ribbon running underneath the label. Press down evenly for a smooth appearance.

9. Insert CD into pocket.

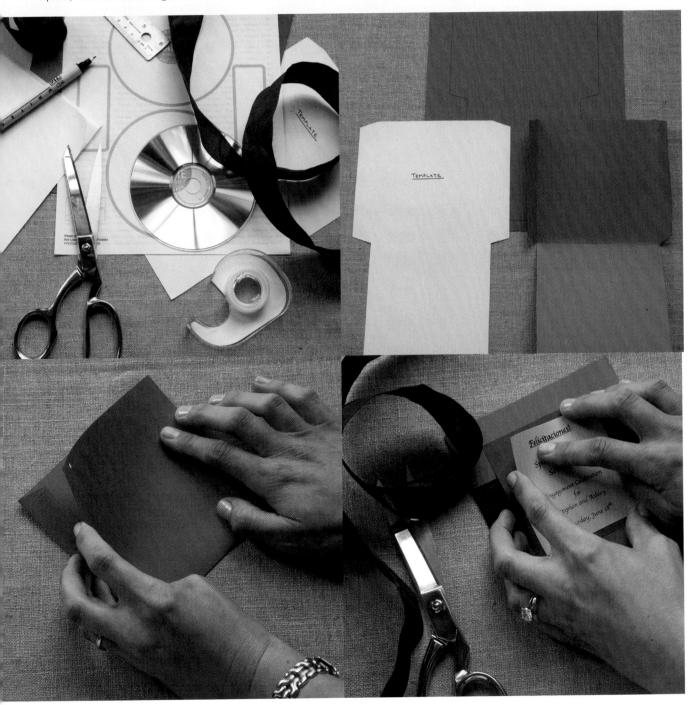

If you want to get creative, make something from scratch. Whether the favor is rolled beeswax candles or castile soaps, cookies, miniloaf cakes, or anything you baked, people love to get homemade things. That someone took the time to make something just for them really makes them feel special.

project SOFTLY SCENTED SACHETS

There are scented sachets in my clothes drawer and in my bathroom linens. I even have them in my craft room but I never realized how important lavender sachets are until I saw lavender sachet key chains for sale in a gift store; you're supposed to inhale deeply when you feel road rage coming on! So maybe we should all keep a lavender sachet in the glove compartment!

Craft stores sell lots of different fillers for sachets but when I make sachets, I always fill them with lavender. I like lavender, it's inexpensive, the fragrance is not overpowering, and it feels good in the sachet. And I usually make the sachets from silk because I love silk and all the vibrant colors it comes in. Thicker fabrics don't allow the fragrance of the filling to come through as well, plus silk has a lovely texture and it's elegant. Sometimes I use one color of silk for the front and a complementary color for the back of each sachet. Though it might seem expensive, you're only using maybe a yard for all your favors. You get this exquisite favor that costs about a dollar; I think that's a lot of luxury for not a lot of money.

Often I make the sachets without any stamped decoration; the pretty fabric and coordinating ribbon are enough.

One of my mottos is "less is often more" and this is one of those times. But when the sachets are for a themed party, whether it's a girlfriends get-together or a wedding shower, I do like to use a stamp. I have a stamp that reads "amore," and I just love to use that one for wedding showers. Craft stores have so many great rubber stamps to choose from; it's fun to search for the right message or image.

The fragrance always stays
in the hand that gives the rose. HADA BEJAR

JUST FOR YOU

WHAT YOU'LL NEED

EQUIPMENT

- Scissors
- Sewing machine
- Needle and thread
- Iron

MATERIALS

- $1/4$ yard fabric, preferably silk, in coordinating color
- Pins
- Sheet of paper
- Rubber stamp and fabric stamp pad (optional)
- 2 cups lavender or other fragrant dried herbs
- 1 yard ribbon

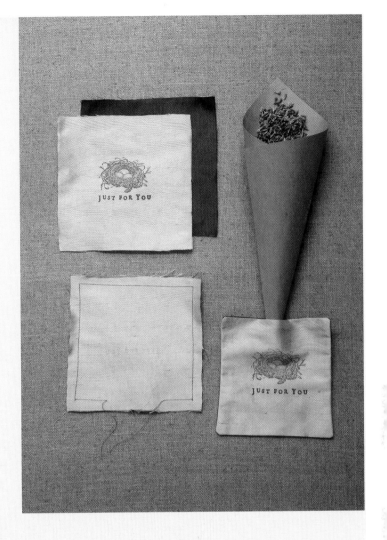

WHAT YOU'LL DO

1. Cut out two 4¾-inch squares from each color of fabric. Take one square of each color, place right sides face-to-face and pin together. Stitch by hand or use a sewing machine around the perimeter of the square, allowing for a ³⁄₈-inch seam; leave 1 inch open on one side. Repeat with other two squares.

2. Turn both the sewn squares inside out and press with a steam iron.

3. If desired, use stamp and stamp pad to stamp image on one side of each sachet.

4. Create a cone-shape funnel with a sheet of paper and pour 1 cup of lavender florets into each sewn square. Finish each sachet by turning selvage under on 1-inch opening and whipstitch closed.

5. Tie the two sachets together with ribbon as if you were wrapping ribbon around a package. Finish with a bow at top.

Note: A quarter yard of fabric will make more than two sachets (makes two sachets, for two sachets per guest).

Many favors, everything from softly scented sachets to the place-card picture frames, appeal to women more than men; I figure that the guys hand their favor over to the girls once they get home. That's fine because you really can't have too many sachets. (Well, maybe the guys put them in their sock drawers, I'm not sure.) Why don't I make one favor for men and one for women? Honestly—it's just too much to do. When I have a games night, I find the boys love the favors—things like a deck of cards wrapped in a red bandana for a Wild West poker party—more than girls, and often if the favor is food, then the man eats more than his fair share.

When you present favors to guests is up to you. You may choose to put the favors on the table at a sit-down dinner. That's what I did with the place-card picture frame favors for the Little Black Dress party because they were also serving as place cards, but even if the favors don't have a job to do, you might like to incorporate them into your table setting. For buffets and drinks parties, I display the favors in a wire basket or bin of some kind in the foyer so everyone sees them as they are heading out the door. No one minds when you hand out the favors. Honestly, any favor you provide will delight your guests—after all, it's an unexpected treat!

MORE JEWELS

Most often when I give favors, they're an end-of-the-night treat that everyone gets as they are leaving. For the Little Black Dress Dinner Party I choose to make the favor do double duty. The mini picture frames I bought and decorated are a favor I've done before; usually I'll put quotes in each frame for fun. I could just have had them on the foyer table for everyone to take home, but I thought it would be really great to put them to work and use them as place-card holders on the dinner table. It was another way of making the table really dressed to the nines. And I thought it would make the favor seem even more special as it had played a part in the evening.

Thinking about the table I'd planned for the dinner, I soon realized that I had to paint the frame with the same colors that would be on the table. Even if it looked beautiful, a red picture frame would have stuck out so much, all eyes would have been on it rather than delighting in the table as a whole. So I used oyster white, pewter, and black, the main colors of the table settings, and I bought pearlescent paints which made the frames seem so much fancier than regular flat paint would have done. That and adding the button really played off the string-of-pearls napkin ring and I think it added to the bejeweled feeling of the evening.

project PLACE CARD PICTURE FRAME

For several years I've used mini-frames as place-card holders for some of my parties. People often commented how cute they were and I thought I should make ones that everyone could take home! So I did. The frames I use for place card holders are silver but for a party favor I wanted something more jazzed up (and not as expensive!), a plain wooden frame is just the thing, it's easy to dress up.

To use the frames as favors for a buffet or other party where you don't need place cards, simply find a great quote, type it up on the computer, and size it to fit the frame—or copy it out by hand if you have great handwriting. Remember that what you put in the frame is not supposed to be permanent; the frames are for your guests to display a favorite image in. Also keep this in mind when choosing a rubber stamp to decorate the frame: I always go for something elegant and sophisticated. Even if the frame is the favor for a baby shower, I use a flourish design, not a baby carriage stamp, because the frame is a gift for the guest and I want her to be able to display it anywhere.

WHAT YOU'LL NEED

EQUIPMENT

- Sponge roller
- Paint brush
- Computer and printer
- Scissors

MATERIALS

- Flat bordered 2 x 3-inch wooden frame
- 150-grit sandpaper
- Acrylic paint in two contrasting colors

- Decorative foam stamp
- Glue gun and glue sticks or clear drying glue
- 2–3 mm rhinestones
- 4-inch piece of 1-inch-wide ribbon
- Button
- Decorative printer-friendly paper

Note: This project can also be made using a rubber stamp and ink pad in place of foam stamp and one color of acrylic paint.

WHAT YOU'LL DO

1. Remove glass and frame backing. Sand front and sides of frame with sandpaper. Wipe to remove any dust.

2. Use sponge roller to paint frame and allow to dry. Apply second coat and let dry.

3. Brush contrasting paint on foam stamp and apply to front of frame.

4. Glue small rhinestones on inner portion of frame.

5. Knot ribbon in the middle and glue ribbon by its knot to top front of frame. Trim ends of ribbon to desired length. Glue button on top of knot.

6. Type quote or guest's name on computer and print on decorative paper. Trim paper to fit inside frame.

7. Place printed portion behind glass and reassemble frame.

Journal Entry

Jot ideas for party favors, and how to wrap them, in your journal. Also keep a note of sources and prices of favors, materials to make favors, and wrappings as it's easy to lose phone numbers or addresses or forget where you saw the perfect bags.

CHAPTER 12

Countdown TO THE Party

Hosting a party is a little like putting on a play—the planning, the producing, the casting—only instead of actors you're choosing which recipes and tableware will get the starring roles. The production team is smaller, so you are producer and stage manager plus you have the leading role. There's no dress rehearsal but you may have butterflies in your stomach before the curtain goes up and the guests arrive. Don't let first-night nerves get you into a lather. As opening night approaches the pressure builds and it's easy to forget your game plan and, well, just panic—that is not a good thing to do. Stick to that clever game plan you made and aim to do as much as possible before the day of the party.

A week or more before the party consider what I call logistics: parking, pets, kids, and neighbors. The key to logistics, like so much else, is timing—arrange everything ahead of time and do as much as you can as far ahead as possible.

Let the neighbors, the doorman, gatemaster of your subdivision, or anyone else who might be affected by the party, know that you are expecting company. If you're having a larger gathering, inviting the neighbors is a good way to ease any potential irritations. Telling everyone ahead of time, at least a week, preferably when you receive your first RSVPs, prevents last-minute problems. Plan parking; work it out so that you won't cut off access to neighbors' property or inconvenience anyone. If your pet isn't the party type or you have guests coming who are allergic, arrange for your dog or cat to have a playdate with your parents or a day at the kennel. Unless they really are Mom's little helpers, arrange for the kids to go to Grandma's or on a playdate. And if the date can start in the morning of the day of the party, not just before the party starts, you'll have more time to scrub the scuff marks off the wall.

Send In the Reinforcements

Many entertaining books talk about hiring help but few people I know spend their hard-earned cash on caterers or a clean-up crew when they're having a party. Assign some duties to your partner or spouse; perhaps he can be bartender or at least offer everyone a first drink or be responsible for introducing guests to one another when you return to the kitchen to finish dinner preparations. If your children are old enough, they can be in charge of coat check or passing the hors d'oeuvres. (This isn't necessary but guests are often charmed by a young waiter and the "waiter" feels proud for helping.) If a friend offers to come by early to help, ask her to bring the ice for the drinks, two great big helps for the hostess at the eleventh hour.

SETTING UP

Having already planned where you'll be serving drinks and food and how many chairs you require or need to remove from the party room, you should (if you can) arrange the furniture for the party about three days before the party. At the same time, set up the dinner table or buffet and the bar or drinks table. A dinner table setting is fairly straightforward; you know what the menu is and what utensils you need for each course plus you've worked out your centerpiece and any other elements of decadence or fun you're including. The buffet will require a little more strategizing. Arrange the serving platters so they look good and are accessible to guests; keep to a minimum the need to reach over dishes to avoid sleeves trailing through food or things getting knocked to the floor. Putting Post-it notes on each platter or table location is a great way to remember what food goes where, and don't forget to include appropriate serving utensils for each dish; set them right beside the dish. There's no reason to wait till the last minute to set the table; eat at the kitchen counter or in front of the TV between now and the party. Don't put off setting the table unless you're sheet rocking your house and it's just too dusty to leave a plate out for two days! (But you wouldn't schedule a party when you're doing major home renovations, would you?)

*Isn't elegance forgetting
what one is wearing?*

YVES ST. LAURENT

HAVEN'T GOT A THING TO WEAR?

The what-to-wear dilemma—solve this way ahead of the day of the party. Pick out your ensemble, try it on with the shoes and accessories you'll wear, and work out how you'll fix your hair. There's no time in the day-of-the-party game plan for trying to find an outfit.

The day of the party is also not the time to schedule spa treatments but you do want to allow for a shower and getting dressed, made up, and hair done; you might like to add this to your game plan to make sure you have time. Some people can shower in the morning and after an afternoon of preparty prep they still look fresh. Not me. I always aim to shower two hours before the party, though often find it gets pushed back to one hour before—I'll be working in the kitchen and think "just fifteen more minutes" and that "fifteen more minutes" leads to another fifteen until I finally end up showering an hour before the party starts. If something happens and there just isn't time for a shower, don't feel bad. Instead pull out your favorite perfume, a spritz of scent as you pull on your clothes in record time will help you feel revived and ready to go.

In my rule book, you should be dressed a minimum of thirty minutes before the appointed hour, then you are ready to face the world should guests start arriving early. Early arrivers can join the beautifully turned-out you in the kitchen as you do the final prep—much better that than they spend time in the kitchen with your beautifully presented hors d'oeuvres as you hurriedly pull on your party frock and skip the makeup because you're too harassed and don't feel there is time to get ready properly. Once dressed, cover your party attire with a full-length apron camouflage before you start to put hors d'oeuvres on platters or get into other potentially sticky situations.

CLEANING UP

During the afternoon before the party, check that the bathroom looks as good as it did when you cleaned it two days ago; sparkling faucets, fresh soap and towels, that four-star hotel style. Vacuum as much or as little as you like. I advise erring on the little side believing that with the lights on dimmers, delectable hors d'oeuvres, amusing conversation, and fifteen other guests traversing the rug, no one will notice if it wasn't immaculate at the get-go. Plus the less time spent with the vacuum the more time there is to devote to dinner prep.

Just as meal preparation benefits from advanced planning, so does cleanup. A bit of organization, like cleaning as you cook rather than saving a great stack of pots and pans, can make it go faster and more easily. Make sure the kitchen is wiped down after you finish all the cooking, run the dishwasher and empty it before your guests arrive. That way you can easily place your stacked dirty dishes inside it. Once your guests leave, remove the stacked dishes, rinse them, and load them properly. Organize an area for glassware, either loaded in the top of the dishwasher or on a piece of countertop separate from other tableware where it is less likely to get tipped over or broken. Place a trash bin ready so you can scrape dishes into it as you bring them into the kitchen.

THE LITTLE BLACK DRESS DINNER PARTY COUNTDOWN

So it's three o'clock on the day of the party. I'm a bit messy and looking forward to taking a shower. Things are coming together pretty well. I set the table two days ago and it still looks good. That's one advantage to having a nonfloral centerpiece; my candles and greenery look just as fresh as when I assembled them. I'm just finishing up cutting out the pumpernickel squares in the kitchen. I'm actually really enjoying prepping this meal. There was a lot I was able to do ahead; I made the salmon mixture for the hors d'oeuvres yesterday and even put it in a piping bag with the tip on. I wrapped the tip so it wouldn't dry out and put it in the refrigerator. I'll assemble the hors d'oeuvres just before everyone comes. I made the appetizer tartlet shells, baked them yesterday, and made the filling for them last night, and that's in the fridge too, in a pitcher ready to pour into the shells and bake, half an hour before everyone is due. In fact the fridge is a little full right now; the lamb racks are also in there. I applied the herb rub and refrigerated them last night. I'll take them out of the refrigerator so they have time to come to room temperature before I sear them. They'll go in the oven just before the party starts. When they are resting after roasting, I'll make the red wine reduction sauce.

Dividing the preparations for this meal over several days, outlining what to do when in my party timeline, and doing most of the real work well before today means I'm not feeling overwhelmed or overtired now, just a little hungry—I could eat some hors d'oeuvres right now. I made the vinai-grette three days ago and could have made it even earlier. The herbs for the lamb rub were chopped two days ago. This menu is very accommodating; the dishes don't have to be served piping hot so I could have baked the tartlets earlier this afternoon, or even this morning, and tented them with foil. Even the lamb is easy going. It will sit and rest for twenty minutes once it's finished cooking, but if it sits for forty minutes in a foil tent, that's fine too.

Some things cannot be done ahead, like washing the salad, which I'll do once the tartlets have come out of the oven and are cooling. I serve them at room temperature, which makes it easier than having to pull them out of the oven and serve them once everyone is at the table. Also if they are too hot they'll wilt the salad, which wouldn't look very appetizing. And to avoid greens soggy from sitting in dressing, I won't dress the salad until I'm ready to serve the appetizer. The vegetables are easy to prepare but taste best if made close to dinner so I'll cook them right before I wash the salad. To ensure the Mini Molten Chocolate Cakes are truly molten, they need to be baked just before serving. The batter is very forgiving so I made and divided it between the prepared mini-Bundt pans this morning, then covered them with plastic wrap and stored them in the refrigerator. I just need to remember to take them from the refrigerator about half an hour before baking. The Champagne for my signature drink, the Panache, plus the white wine, soda, and mineral water are already in the fridge.

*Find something you're passionate about
and keep tremendously interested in it.*

JULIA CHILD

Around five I'll do a walk-through and pick up anything that's still lying around so the house looks more presentable. That, plus spot-cleaning the kitchen, bathroom touch-ups, and dimming the lights takes care of the cleanup. Then into the shower and my own little black dress. Yes, I'm dressing to match the theme of the dinner!

THE TWENTY-MINUTES-TO-GO CHECKLIST

This is my essential last-minute helpmate. Twenty minutes before company is coming, I run through these questions in my head. Doing this sets my mind at ease, quells that "what have I forgotten?" panic. Try it and I'm sure you'll find it works like a charm for you too.

Check that:

- Candles are lit.
- Outdoor/front patio lights are on.
- Coat closet or another spot is cleared and ready to accept coats, purses, and other personal items.
- Indoor lighting is adjusted properly.
- Music is playing.
- Wine is opened and the white is chilling, along with other drinks, in ice.
- The hors d'oeuvres are ready on platters (or baking or reheating in the oven).
- The kitchen is wiped down and spot-cleaned.
- Do a quick walk-through of the house, checking the dining table or buffet, powder room, and kitchen to make sure everything is in its place and looks ready.
- You are completely dressed, accessorized, and ready to greet your guests.
- Take a deep breath, look around at the wonderful party setting you've created, smile—you are ready for the fun!

IT'S FINE, REALLY IT IS

Pace yourself; if you feel overwhelmed check your game plan and make sure you're on track. Even if you find you are running behind schedule, take a moment, breath some deep yogic breaths, or put on a favorite CD (and sing along) while you work. Pour yourself a glass of wine to enjoy as you work—but don't drain the bottle before everyone arrives!

It took me a while to work out that it's no use getting frazzled. I used to panic and go into hyperdrive at the eleventh hour. Experience has taught me that you don't have to go mad; you don't even have to get everything done on time. I bet even Martha has answered the door with wet hair. No matter how good you are or how often you entertain, things can go wrong. As long as you can hand your guests something to drink and you are pleasant and presentable that's enough. Think gracious hostess; your attitude is more important than your barbecued salmon.

CHAPTER 13

AN AFFAIR TO
Remember

The moment the doorbell rings you're in hostess mode. No longer the party planner, decorator, and chef, you're now the gracious hostess attending to the needs of your guests and making sure everyone (including yourself) has a good time. Entertaining is a bit like being onstage. When guests arrive it's as if the curtain has been raised and there you are, center stage, wanting to please your audience. Try to be relaxed so you don't project a feeling of tension and channel any nervousness you feel into energy and direct it to action, taking coats, getting drinks, and, more than anything else, spending time with your guests.

Sometimes you have to create what you want to be a part of. GERI WEITZMAN

There is a delicate balance between enjoying yourself and taking care of your guests and over time I've learned to err on the side of enjoying myself. If it seems that you, the hostess, are not having fun, you're rushing around filling glasses and replenishing platters, then your guests feel uptight. It's best to let glasses get a little empty and actually have a laugh with your friends; remember you are the hostess not a servant. As you gain confidence in your entertaining skills, you'll get a better sense of this. For now, realize that if you're sweating you're probably trying too hard!

MEET AND GREET

Who hasn't been to a party where they feel horribly self-conscious and insecure when they arrive? This is perhaps the most important time to make your guests feel comfortable. Even if you are behind schedule—and it happens sometimes—make time to greet your guests at the door with a big smile. As with job interviews, the first impression counts. If you really must leave the door, get your partner or a good friend to stand in for a few minutes.

Ask early-arriving guests to join you in the kitchen for a drink, then you can continue to prep and they'll feel more at ease than they would alone in the party room. Fetch guests a first drink and point the way to the bar so they can help themselves to more later. Also show them where the food is.

THE MILD-MANNERED HOSTESS

HOW TO ACCEPT HOSTESS GIFTS POLITELY

Some guests will bring hostess gifts, so it's a good idea to plan a place to put them. You don't have to open a hostess gift when you receive it. Simply thank the guest and place it somewhere out of the way, but not out of sight. I usually don't open a wrapped gift until after the party and place any gifts I receive on a kitchen countertop that's away from the food prep area. A sideboard or desk in part of the house where the party is taking place is also a good spot; there gifts are on display but not in the way. Don't put gifts on a foyer table where they might act as a nasty reminder to other guests because they didn't bring anything—they didn't have to and you don't want to make them feel bad.

WHAT IF GUESTS BRING WINE?

If you are given a bottle of wine, you may choose to open it and serve it at your party but you certainly don't have to. If it's something really super you might want to be selfish and save it for yourself for later! If you think it might not taste that good or really doesn't complement the meal, then reserve it for future use. A guest should not force you to open any wine they bring; a gift of wine is intended as a gift, not as a supplement to your party.

HOW TO HANDLE GIFTS OF FLOWERS

While I think fresh flowers are beautiful they can be a bit of a hassle as a hostess gift. What was intended as a thoughtful gift becomes a time-consuming project, one that needs to be tended to immediately. Later I'll enjoy having them but in the heat of the party as everyone's arriving, it's hard to make time to deal with them when I want to be greeting everyone and getting them drinks. To make it easier to handle floral gifts, I keep a vase easily accessible. Flowers require water so leaving them in their paper on the countertop is not an option; you must at least quickly put them in water and ideally find a place to display them, so as not to offend the guest who brought them.

When you are the guest, my advice is not to bring fresh flowers as a hostess gift. If flowers are your thing send them to the hostess a day or two before her party. That way she has time to arrange them, incorporate them into her décor, and admire your thoughtful gift.

WHAT IF SOMEONE BRINGS FOOD (AND IT'S NOT A POTLUCK PARTY)?

If guests bring food, whether it's a homemade dip and crudités or store-bought cheese and crackers, whether it works with your menu or not, thank them, remark on

Too much of a good thing can be wonderful.

MAE WEST

how delicious it looks, and set it out. If they brought something that needs plating, go ahead and use one of your platters, but if the dish comes already on a platter, set it out on that platter. I admit to having a hard time with this. I would love to use my own serve ware so it fits in with the look of the buffet, rather than sticking out, but I know that's bad form. If the dish really doesn't go with the rest of the food, set it in its own "special" place, a little out of the main traffic area. However, when someone arrives with a platter of cookies and rearranges your carefully laid out spread, dumping her contribution in the center of the entrées, then I think it's fine to move them, explaining that it's not dessert time yet.

Even though etiquette is on the side of the hardworking hostess, ruling that the hostess doesn't have to serve unrequested food a guest may bring, I learned to soften my attitude after being on the receiving side of the ire of an uptight hostess when I took cookies to a party. So now, although I like things to be just as I've planned, I know not to make it clear that I didn't wish for this food.

TOP UPS

While mingling and talking, be on the lookout for empty glasses and ask their owners if you can get them another. You'll probably find that once you've got them an initial drink, most guests will wander over and refill their own glasses, but it's good to ask, if you notice an empty or nearly empty glass. If someone does need another drink, usually I find he comes with me to the bar when I take his glass, and guys often insist they make their own drink.

HAVE AN HORS D'OEUVRE

Don't worry about passing the hors d'oeuvres. If you're having eight for dinner everyone can see and help themselves. When it's a larger party, you could take a platter and pass through the room but usually I don't do this—I concentrate on making sure everyone has a drink and leave them to find their own way to the eats. Also I don't like to force food on people; they may not want to eat at that moment but may feel obligated to take something if I'm pushing a tray in their faces.

Party Barometer/Atmosphere Check

Once the party is under way, do an atmosphere check. Just step back from the room and listen—is the music at the right level? Now that the room is full of people talking it may seem too quiet or too loud. Is the lighting right— not too bright, or too dark? Are there enough glasses on the bar?

At the same time survey the room and make sure that no one is left out of the conversation. If you notice someone or a couple who are by themselves and look a little lost, go over and talk to them; bring them into the party by introducing them to others.

COME AND GET IT

Everything is going great, everyone is having a good time; maybe they're having too good a time because no one has noticed you've arrived with the hot appetizers, just out of the oven and at their peak. This happens; don't get cross, don't start bellowing that the food is ready, don't force people to eat. Just announce, "The appetizers are hot, eat them before they get cold." I find it helps if I take one and pop it into my mouth; no one wants to be first and seeing you eating helps get the idea over that they can join in. With a buffet, I serve the entrées on the table where the appetizers were, so guests will see me collecting all the appetizer platters and bringing out the sides and mains. If that doesn't attract a couple of hungry guests, plate in hand, then I say, "Dinner is served," and round up someone, usually Todd, to be first in line because once someone starts to help himself, a line forms quickly.

As there are fewer guests for a sit-down, it's easier to spread the word that it's time to come to the table. I'll just say, "Okay, let's go eat," and point the way to the dining room. For a casual sit-down meal, I'll have water in the water glasses and, if there's a salad course, the salad plated at each place so the meal is ready to start. Some guests may notice this before I ask them to come to table. If I've set a more formal table with place cards and napkins on the chargers, then after everyone has been seated and taken her napkin, I'll bring in the salad plates.

SERVING AND CLEARING

Remember the rule "Serve from the left, clear from the right"? It still holds true but there are exceptions, so don't sweat it. It's more important that you are at ease and everyone is having fun than for you to serve the meal like a professional. Both etiquette and common sense say you should never reach through guests engaged in conversation; serve or clear from the other side. Wine is generally served from the right because a wineglass is placed on the right side.

After the main course, all tableware including salt and pepper shakers, bread and butter plates, and chargers should be cleared but napkins and silverware for dessert remain. If a wineglass is empty I take it away; if it's half full I'll leave it on the table. If I'm going to serve a dessert wine I'll tell my guests that and ask if they would like to keep their other wine.

STACK AND GO

Some people say you should clean up as the party progresses but I never do. Yes, take abandoned glasses and empty platters to the kitchen but never start doing the dishes or loading the dishwasher during the party. To me it's just plain bad manners to start cleaning up while you still have company. Seeing you slaving will either make guests feel awkward, as if you want them to leave, or make them feel they should pitch in, which they shouldn't—they are at the party to have fun and not become the cleaning crew. Collect and stack dirty plates in the kitchen, use the dishwasher or a cool oven as a holding tank so the kitchen doesn't seem chaotic.

Even if something gets spilled, I try to keep it in perspective and not make a big fuss. Dry up a spill and do the minimum to prevent it from staining. Save stain treatment for later.

HOW DO YOU DEAL WITH OFFERS OF HELP FROM GUESTS?

If you'd like help, accept and tell them how they can help you. If you don't want help, politely refuse. If someone sees me carrying plates or platters to the table and offers to help, that's great. I accept readily but I don't let guests start cleaning up. Even if they insist they want to, I refuse and explain that I want them to have fun at my party and I don't want to clean up right now so I certainly don't want them to be cleaning up. Often I'll say, "No way, let's go get a glass of wine instead."

WHAT TO DO IF YOU RUN OUT OF DRINKS?

I've run out of drinks before; it's a horrible thing to happen. Someone has to go to the store and get more. The experience taught me never to skimp, to buy twice as much as I think I need. Beer or soda will keep for several months, wine and liquor for much longer, so it's best to stock up and avoid such embarrassments. If you do run out of, say, white wine and it's late and the wine store has closed, don't feel bad. You've done your job; encourage guests to move to another beverage—or maybe it's time that everyone thought about going home!

THE END OF THE AFFAIR

All good things must come to an end. You're operating on hostess high, a kind of adrenalin, but maybe you are feeling tired and it is late. If you decide it is time to bring the party to a close there are subtle things you can do to indicate it's time everyone went home. I turn things down a notch by turning lights down or up to bright. I might turn the music off, or my favorite prompt is to blow out candles; that's a pretty definite indication that the party is over. If they still don't take the hint, I tell them, "I'm exhausted, I'd love to stay and chat but I've got to go to bed. Let's do this again soon."

Even if you are tired, don't forget to remind guests to take their party favors when you wish them good-bye. If it's a favor like the picture frame place card that was on the table during dinner, then everyone has already seen it and knows it's their favor but may well forget to take it home. If favors are in the foyer and they need to pick one up from there, tell them that.

Something special happens at a party when there's a meal ahead and many friends around; it's a special sort of magic so enjoy it while it's happening. Somewhere between the hellos and the first glass of wine and the hugs and sleepy good-byes, be sure to stand back and admire the scene you created. Feast upon the celebration of people and good times.

PLENTY OF PANACHE

Phew, I mean that in a good way. I am tired but also a bit wired. It's midnight and Ashley and Stephen left about ten minutes ago and they were the last to leave (as always!). It went well, it really did, and it was fun. Everyone had a Panache and seemed to really dig it; in fact, Stephen quickly picked up on how to prepare it and made me one while I was taking the lamb out of the oven!

I thought the table looked really magical, so sparkly—just how I'd hoped it would. When I entertain more casually, I plate the salad before everyone sits down. Tonight I got everyone to come to the table before I brought in the salad. That way they saw the table before the food came in. So they sat down and picked up their menus, one at each place, took their napkins, then I swooped in and took their salad plates to the kitchen where I put some salad on each plate—with tongs it's so easy—placed a tartlet besides the greens, and was ready to go.

The food went well, too well maybe. David asked for another tartlet after he'd wolfed the first. I felt complimented that he liked it so much but it caused a dilemma I'd never come up against before—there weren't any extras. What with making sure everyone has everything he needs, I was a bit slower than the others in eating mine and still had half left, so jokingly I offered him the half I hadn't eaten—and he took it!

The lamb tasted better than any time I'd made it before. I think that was because it went so well with the red wine—boy, was that good. Even Stephen who probably knows more about wine than any of our other friends remarked on how great it was. I was worried they'd drink my share while I was plating the lamb in the kitchen! Luckily everyone was busy reading the quotes I'd hidden under each dinner plate. They were revealed when I took the now empty salad plates away and removed the dinner plates at the same time—saving myself one trip to and from the kitchen with that crafty move. The quotes were a great success; everyone was laughing. Think I really picked the right one for Ashley. Stephen was still ribbing her about it when we went into the family room after dessert. Yum, that dessert was a real winner too; everyone was impressed with the individual presentation and you should have seen Kevin scraping his plate to get all the chocolate! I'm happy but ready for bed!

CHAPTER 14

Bringing IT ALL Together

It's over, it was great, now I'm ready for more. It's true, I do get a buzz from entertaining and creating and sharing special times with friends and family. Now that you've followed my progress as I planned and pulled off that truly special Little Black Dress Dinner Party and gotten into the excitement of entertaining, I wanted to show you how, with your expanding entertaining savvy and your basic arsenal, there are so many varied kinds of parties you can host. It's that old idea of once you know the basics you can run with it. In this chapter you'll see four other quite different parties I've hosted recently: a super-easy wine and cheese tasting party, a buffet to celebrate an engagement, a daytime baby shower, and a casual supper in the kitchen. Consider these parties ideas and inspirations. Take what you like and go with it. Pare them down; if you don't want to make cupcakes, buy them, or scale them up, double the recipes, and invite more guests. The door to entertaining is open, now go through it.

WINE AND CHEESE PARTY

Who: Eight friends who don't already know each
   other but should

When: Saturday at 7:30 P.M.

Where: Kitchen and family room

What I'm wearing: Sexy top, cool pants; we're going
   on out to dinner, the night is young. . . .

Soundtrack: Swing and standards

Favor: Wood-handled corkscrew with printed paper
   cocktail napkins tied with raffia

MENU

Wine	*Cheese*
Viognier (California)	Stilton
Petite Syrah (California)	Comte
Barolo (Italy)	St. André
	Assorted crackers

As I'm not a big cocktail drinker but love wine, it's often the focus of my entertaining and never more so than when I host a wine and cheese party. Not a retro cheese-on-sticks kind of thing, this is an intimate yet casual party that I can put together quickly. There's no cooking, just shopping for the right cheese and crackers to serve with the wines I've chosen. It's deliberately simple because we're eating dinner out afterward. If we weren't eating out I'd add nuts, olives, cured meats, and fruit to complement the cheese selections.

This kind of party is easy to throw for a larger group—more wine, more cheese, more glasses, and more plates and you're set. I really enjoy choosing the wine and cheese and try to pick something a little out of the ordinary—no California Chardonnay here but a Viognier from the golden state, no brie but maybe a decadent triple crème cheese like Saint-André. For this particular party I went with one white and two reds but it could be all white wine or all red, all French wine and French cheese, all Australian selections, the permutations are endless. No matter what is served the concept remains the same, it's kind of a widen-your-horizons, try-something-a-bit-new type party. Each cheese is identified by a small card-stock card, similar to

the ones I use to identify dishes for a buffet, only this time I use corks split horizontally as card holders. The chalkboard acts as an informal menu.

The tasting sheets I made on the computer with vintage illustrations echoing those on the invitations aren't for a formal, stuffy taste-and-spit type of thing; they're for anyone to jot down the name of a wine they liked or even the phone number of the couple they just met! And because it's a casual tasting party, everyone sticks with the same glass when they try the different wines—the dishwasher loves that!

I put the cheese and crackers on my wooden cheese board and used wooden cocktail plates. I could have used the arsenal cocktail plates but I went with the wooden ones because I liked the way they echoed the other wooden accents of the party, the wooden cheese board and the wood-handled corkscrew favor. Both the cheese and the wine were set up along with glasses and plates on the kitchen island. The idea is to drink and taste whatever you like, try all three wines or just drink one. Each time I have a party like this, friends discover a wine they like so much they go out and buy a case of it, or they find a new cheese they want to eat every day.

SPANISH BUFFET

Who: Sixteen guests ranging in age from twenty-one
    to fifty-five

When: Saturday at 6:30 P.M.

Where: Family room

What I'm wearing: Something brightly colored, a big
    skirt perhaps

Soundtrack: Spanish guitar, Segovia

Favor: CD of Spanish guitar music in a terra-cotta
    and red card-stock envelope wrapped with
    ribbon

When Ashley and Stephen got engaged I knew I'd need to host their engagement party. She's a really good friend and his family lives in Ireland so none of them were around to do the party. The idea for the food came from Ashley's love of bright orange, gold, and brown. When I thought of those colors, I remembered this "Spanish" Madame Alexander doll I had as a kid and thought about a Spanish motif for the party using Ashley's colors. Then I remembered she loves mussels too, and thought of making paella which has mussels and so many other lovely ingredients, plus it worked with the Spanish idea. Best of all, I've made paella many times before and though it needs to be made close to the time of the party, you can separate out all the chopping and measuring so the actual preparation is not as lengthy. Tres leches cake is more Mexican than Spanish but it rounded out the menu perfectly. Also when I plan a party or a meal, I don't want everything to be so matchy-matchy; if there is a theme it should be subtle or fun.

Even though this party is for sixteen, I use real plates and silverware and cloth napkins. When I invite people to my house, whether it's for an engagement, a birthday, a holi-day, or just because I want to, it should be special and paper or plastic plates and silverware just don't feel good. Plus they can be difficult to eat from particularly if you're standing and eating as you might do at a buffet. So I buy lots of inexpensive plates; it's an initial investment but one that pays off in the long haul. And for a buffet, I always use descriptive dish cards so everyone knows what's on each platter, in case it's something they don't like or are allergic to. For this buffet, I made the cards using my favorite layered card-stock technique in the party colors.

When you're feeding more mouths, as happens with a buffet, it's especially important that the food can be made ahead or all the prep work done ahead so the actual cooking is relatively rapid. For this meal, I made the tres leches cake and both the filling and the dough for the empanadas the day before. I couldn't decide whether to order the shellfish at the fish market and pick it up on the day of the party or buy it the day before to avoid extra running around on the day of the party. Either would work but eventually I went with buying it the day before. The following recipes serve sixteen but they can be halved or quartered for a smaller gathering.

RECIPES

SPICED PORK EMPANADAS

DOUGH

4 cups all-purpose flour

$1\frac{1}{2}$ teaspoons kosher salt

12 ounces (3 sticks) unsalted butter, cubed and
   chilled

8 ounces cream cheese, cubed and chilled

1 egg yolk combined with 2 teaspoons ice water

2 eggs lightly whisked with 2 teaspoons cold water,
   for egg wash

$\frac{1}{2}$ cup sliced almonds (for tops of empanadas)

FILLING

2 tablespoons olive oil

$\frac{3}{4}$ pound ground pork

Kosher salt

1 large onion, diced

5 cloves garlic, minced

2 teaspoons Spanish paprika (or to taste)

2 tablespoons tomato paste

$\frac{1}{2}$ cup pitted green olives, coarsely chopped

$\frac{1}{4}$ cup golden raisins

$\frac{1}{4}$ cup hot water

3 hard-boiled eggs, coarsely chopped

$\frac{1}{2}$ cup parsley, coarsely chopped

Freshly ground black pepper

FOR THE DOUGH

1. In the bowl of an electric mixer fitted with a paddle attachment, place flour and salt and stir to combine. Add
chilled butter and cream cheese and toss in the flour to
coat. On medium-low speed, work the butter and cream
cheese into the flour until dough appears pebbly. With the
paddle working, drizzle in the egg yolk water and continue
to mix until dough begins to come together into one large
mass. (It may not be necessary to use all of the egg yolk
water; keep a close eye on the dough and stop adding liquid when the large clumps of dough begin to adhere to one
another. Use your hands to press the dough together in the
bowl. If the dough is still dry and not coming together in
large clumps after adding the liquid, add more water, a
teaspoon at a time, until dough begins to come together.)

Gather dough into a ball. Divide into four pieces and form
each into a flattened disc. Wrap each disc tightly in plastic
wrap and allow to rest in the refrigerator for at least an
hour before rolling out. (At this point, the dough may be
stored in the refrigerator for up to two days or in the freezer
for one month.)

2. Working with one disc of dough at a time, roll into an
$\frac{1}{8}$-inch-thick circle. Using a round 3-inch biscuit or
cookie cutter, cut out eight circles of dough and transfer
them to a baking sheet. Place baking sheet in the refrigerator and repeat rolling and cutting for each of the remaining
three discs of dough. You will have a total of thirty-two
3-inch circles.

FOR THE FILLING

1. Heat oil over medium-high heat in a medium-sized sauté pan. When oil is shimmering add pork, breaking it into little clumps with your fingers as you add it to the pan. (Take care not to crowd the pan; it may be necessary to sear the meat in two batches.) Allow meat to brown for a few minutes before stirring. Add a few pinches of salt and continue browning until most of the pork has a golden brown crust, adjusting heat as necessary. Remove meat from pan with a slotted spoon and set aside in a bowl.

2. Add onion to pan and stir quickly to help release the browned bits from the bottom of the pan. Reduce heat to medium, add a generous pinch of salt, and sauté onion until thoroughly soft and translucent, 7–10 minutes. Add garlic and cook for another few minutes, stirring, until garlic is soft and fragrant. Add paprika and stir. Add tomato paste and sauté for a minute until it becomes fragrant. Return pork and any accumulated juices to the pan and stir.

3. Add olives and raisins along with a quarter cup of hot water and increase heat to medium-high. Allow water to nearly evaporate then remove pan from heat. Let cool for a few minutes before stirring in hard-boiled egg and parsley and seasoning with salt and freshly ground pepper. When the filling has cooled to room temperature, transfer to a sealed container and place in the refrigerator for at least an hour. (Filling can be stored, well sealed, in the refrigerator for up to 24 hours.)

FILLING AND BAKING EMPANADILLAS

1. Preheat the oven to 375°F.

2. Working with eight circles of dough at a time, place a heaping teaspoon of filling in the center of each circle. Brush the outer edges of each circle with egg wash and fold them in half to form a half moon; the filling should be snuggly encased in the center. Press edges together firmly with the tines of a fork. Place filled empanadas in the refrigerator while you fill and fold the others.

3. Line two baking sheets with parchment paper or aluminum foil and arrange sixteen empanadas on each. Brush tops with more egg wash, sprinkle with sliced almonds, and place in oven. Bake until tops and bottoms are golden brown and the empanadas have puffed slightly, about 25 minutes. Rotate baking sheets halfway through baking. If sliced almonds appear to be browning too rapidly, remove empanadas from the oven and lay a piece of parchment paper on top of them, then return to oven.

4. Remove baking sheets from oven and allow to cool for a few minutes before serving. (Empanadas may be served warm or at room temperature. They can be baked up to several hours in advance and reheated in a 350°F. oven.)

Makes 32

PAELLA

Originally paella was a dish from the Valencia region of Spain, made with chicken, rabbit, snail, and three different kinds of green beans. Today if you say paella most people think of a dish with seafood, chicken, and vegetables much like this one I like to make. Spanish friends have told me there is no right or wrong recipe for this one-pot feast; there are endless variations. So if you prefer your paella without clams or want more vegetables, make it that way.

This recipe feeds a buffet crowd of 16 and is made in a 22-inch paella pan set over two adjacent burners. Paella pans are available at specialty kitchen equipment stores and at www.spanishtable.com. If you don't have a paella pan, it can be cooked in two batches, dividing the ingredients in half and using two large (10- to 13-inch) skillets.

1 teaspoon saffron threads

16–20 chicken drumettes

1 tablespoon Cajun spice

Kosher salt and freshly ground black pepper

$1/2$ cup olive oil

2 cups chopped onion

8 large cloves garlic, minced

3 pounds tomatoes, peeled, seeded, and coarsely chopped, or 1 28 oz. can whole peeled plum tomatoes, drained and coarsely chopped

6 cups Valencia or Arborio rice

10 cups chicken stock

2 teaspoons salt

$1/2$ teaspoon turmeric

1 12-inch piece dried *chourico* (hot Portuguese sausage) or chorizo, browned and sliced into $1/4$-inch circles

32–35 small clams or cockles, scrubbed

2 red bell peppers, seeded and cut into $1/4$-inch strips

32–35 mussels, scrubbed

$1^{1}/2$ cups frozen peas

16–20 medium shrimp, peeled and de-veined

$1/4$ cup olive or vegetable oil (for sautéing shrimp)

Juice of 1 large lemon, plus 2 lemons cut into 8 sections each (for garnish)

$1/2$ cup chopped parsley (for garnish)

1. In a small sauté pan set over medium heat, toast the saffron threads for about 20 seconds or until they begin to curl and uncurl. Transfer the threads to a mortar and pestle and grind to a powder. Pour powder into a measuring cup holding $1^{1}/2$ cups warm water. Stir to dissolve powder.

2. Season chicken with Cajun spice, kosher salt, and pepper.

3. Place the paella pan over two adjacent burners set to medium heat. Heat the oil in the pan until it begins to smoke. Sauté the drumettes in batches until golden brown on all sides, about 5 minutes, adding more oil as necessary. Remove chicken from pan and set aside. Remove or add oil to pan so that about $1/2$ cup remains.

4. In the same pan, still set over medium heat, gently sauté the onion until it is soft and beginning to appear translucent. Add the garlic and cook until it is fragrant, 1–2 minutes more. Add the tomatoes and sauté until their juices have evaporated and the mixture is dry.

5. Increase the heat to medium high and add the rice, stir-

ring to coat it with the oil, making sure the grains are slightly toasted (they will become opaque) before adding the liquid.

6. Add the saffron water, chicken stock, salt, and turmeric to the pan and stir everything until well combined. Bring to a simmer. Place chicken on top of rice (drumettes will be partially submerged in liquid) and lower heat. Allow to simmer for about 18 minutes. (If using two skillets, cover with lids after adding chicken.)

7. Increase heat to medium low. Scatter *chourico* or chorizo, clams, and red pepper strips on top of the chicken and rice and continue to cook until pepper begins to soften and a few clams are beginning to open, about 5 minutes. (Replace lids on skillets.)

8. Add mussels and peas to the pan and cook until all mussels and clams are completely open, another 5–7 minutes. (Tent the pan with a large piece of aluminum foil for a few minutes if the clams and mussels resist opening). Discard any shellfish that remains closed. Remove paella pan from heat.

9. While the clams and mussels are steaming, season shrimp with salt and pepper. Heat ¼ cup oil in a large skillet over medium-high heat until the oil shimmers and begins to smoke. Quickly sauté shrimp, in batches if necessary, until golden. Remove from skillet. Scatter among clams and mussels in paella pan.

10. Sprinkle lemon juice on top of paella and garnish with lemon wedges and parsley just before serving.

Serves 16

TRES LECHES CAKE

CAKE

2 cups all-purpose flour

2 teaspoons baking powder

6 large eggs, separated

2 cups granulated sugar

1 teaspoon pure vanilla extract

½ cup whole milk

RUM MILK SYRUP

1 14-ounce can evaporated milk

1 14-ounce can sweetened condensed milk

1 cup heavy cream

2 tablespoons rum

1 teaspoon pure vanilla extract

MERINGUE ICING

¾ cup granulated sugar

3 large egg whites

FOR THE CAKE

1. Preheat the oven to 350ºF. Butter a 9 x 13-inch baking dish and set aside.
2. Sift together flour and baking powder and set aside.
3. In the bowl of a mixer, beat egg whites on medium speed until soft peaks form. (Take care not to overbeat whites at this stage; they will look grainy and broken.) Add the sugar gradually with the mixer running and beat to stiff, glossy peaks. Add the egg yolks, one by one, beating to incorporate after each addition and scraping down the bowl as needed. Add the vanilla and beat through.
4. Working with a sturdy, long-handled rubber spatula, quickly alternately fold dry ingredients and milk into eggs. Pour batter into prepared dish and use an offset spatula to quickly even out the top. Bake in the center of the oven until golden and a cake tester inserted in the middle of the cake comes out clean, 30–40 minutes.
5. Remove cake from oven and poke holes to the bottom at one-inch intervals.

FOR THE RUM MILK SYRUP

1. Whisk together the evaporated and condensed milks, heavy cream, rum, and vanilla until well combined.
2. While cake is still warm, pour syrup gradually over top of cake, allowing it to soak into holes and down the sides. Let cake cool to room temperature. Cover securely with plastic wrap and place in the refrigerator until well chilled, at least 4 hours or overnight.

FOR THE ICING

1. When the cake is thoroughly chilled, combine ¼ cup water with the sugar in a heavy-bottomed saucepan. Stir and bring to a steady boil over medium-high heat, lower heat slightly when sugar has thoroughly dissolved and, if necessary, swirl pan to reach any grains of sugar clinging to the edges. Boil until syrup reaches the soft-ball stage, 235–240ºF. on a candy thermometer.
2. Meanwhile, in a medium bowl, beat egg whites to soft peaks. When syrup has reached correct temperature, remove from heat. While beating egg whites, pour hot syrup in a slow and steady stream in between the whisk and the side of the bowl. Continue beating until all the syrup has been added and the mixture is cool and glossy.

TO ASSEMBLE

Spread meringue icing evenly across top of the cake. Cut into 16 squares and serve.

Serves 16/makes 16 pieces

A SOUTHERN BABY SHOWER TEA

Who: Twelve girlfriends

When: Sunday at 2 P.M.

Where: Family room

What I'm wearing: A pretty dress

Soundtrack: Sarah McLachlan, Dido, Enya

Favor: Baby bottles filled with almond bath milk

MENU

Specialty Drink: Baby Bellini

Hors d'oeuvres: Spicy Cheese Straws and Candied
    Pecans

Entrée: Assorted tea sandwiches

Dessert: Coconut Cupcakes with White Chocolate
    Frosting

Lunch Beverages: Fresh-Squeezed Lemonade

Tea served with dessert

A few years ago it felt like I went to a baby shower about once a month! Now they aren't so frequent and I enjoy them more. I also enjoy hosting showers because I get to make lots of cute—but not too cute—decorations, like the IT'S A GIRL sign for this party.

On weekends, it just seems too hard to ask people over earlier than two o'clock but two feels like a fine time for a relaxed afternoon party and is perfect for a girly gathering like a baby shower; though an afternoon tea is not strictly for the girls; boys do like tea and cake too!

I used three small tables for the tea because I had them. If I didn't have these round tables I'd likely have used the inexpensive card tables sold at discount stores—with a pretty cloth they'd be perfect. This party would also work well with one larger table for the food and drinks and everyone sitting on the sofa and in various comfy chairs with the food on their laps—I've hosted teas like that before too.

With the tea sandwiches set on the small tables, everyone helped themselves. While they did, I passed around drinks, topping up the Baby Bellinis, and pouring lemonade.

Because it's an afternoon tea, I made several pots of hot tea to accompany the cupcakes for dessert, though this being the South, several guests wanted iced tea.

The basic dinner plates from my entertaining arsenal make a star turn here as chargers under accent cocktail plates that were used for the sandwiches. My favorite project for this party was the stamped dessert plates, made using the cocktail plates from my basic arsenal. They were so easy to make and they look so great no one would ever guess they started life in the dollar store.

It would be quite easy to turn this into a party for more guests; the recipes are easily doubled and the food can be made ahead—well, pretty much everything but the Baby Bellinis, which are a spur-of-the-moment drink. I make the fillings for the sandwiches and the cupcakes the night before, then ice the cakes and make up the sandwiches on the morning of the tea, unless it's a sandwich with a very soggy filling. So making this menu for more guests would be easy—it's mainly a matter of how many teapots you have!

RECIPES

SPICY CHEESE STRAWS

1 cup all-purpose flour

$\frac{1}{2}$ teaspoon baking powder

$\frac{1}{2}$ teaspoon kosher salt

$\frac{1}{2}$ teaspoon cayenne pepper

6 ounces extra-sharp Cheddar cheese, finely grated

2 ounces Parmigiano-Reggiano cheese, finely grated

6 tablespoons (3 ounces) unsalted butter, at room
temperature

1 teaspoon Tabasco sauce

1. Preheat oven to 300ºF. Line two rimmed baking sheets with parchment paper.

2. Sift the flour, baking powder, salt, and cayenne together in a bowl.

3. In another mixing bowl, combine cheeses, butter, and Tabasco thoroughly. Gradually add the dry mixture to the cheese mixture and mix with a stiff rubber spatula or wooden spoon until fully incorporated.

4. Divide dough in half and form each piece into a ball. Cover one ball with plastic wrap and set in a cool part of the kitchen. Lightly flour a clean surface and roll other ball into a 6 x 12-inch rectangle; dough should be approximately $\frac{1}{8}$-inch thick. If necessary, use a pizza cutter to trim edges to an even rectangle.

5. Using the pizza cutter, cut $\frac{1}{3}$-inch strips from the rectangle of dough. Transfer the 6-inch-long straws to the prepared baking sheets, leaving an inch of space between them. Twirl each straw into a loose spiral by gently twisting each strand of dough while lightly pinching the ends between thumb and forefinger. If a strand breaks, simply press it back together with your fingers. Press down firmly on the ends of each straw to anchor them to the parchment.

6. Bake for 15 minutes. Lower the oven temperature to 225ºF. and bake until straws are golden and fragrant, 15–20 minutes more.

7. Remove baking sheets from oven and allow straws to cool completely before transferring to an airtight container.

CANDIED PECANS

$\frac{3}{4}$ cup vegetable oil (such as canola or corn oil)

4 cups pecan halves

3 cups powdered sugar, sifted

2 tablespoons nutmeg

2 tablespoons ground cloves

2 tablespoons cinnamon, plus 1 tablespoon for final
dusting (optional)

1 tablespoon salt

1 teaspoon finely ground black pepper

1. Pour oil into a wide skillet or Dutch oven and heat over medium-low heat for 2 or 3 minutes. Add pecans and toast, stirring constantly, for 15 minutes or until they are cooked through. (Take one out from time to time, let it cool, break it open, and taste.)

2. Mix together the powdered sugar, spices, salt, and pepper in a paper bag and toss to blend.

3. Remove skillet from heat and use a slotted spoon to transfer pecans to a paper towel-lined baking sheet. Allow pecans to cool and dry off for 1–2 minutes, then toss them, in several batches, in the sugar-and-spice bag; make sure pecans are evenly coated. Transfer to a sieve and shake excess seasoning back into the bag.

4. Cool pecans on another baking sheet or large plate. Sift a tablespoon more cinnamon over the nuts, if desired.

FRESH-SQUEEZED LEMONADE

Simple syrup (see recipe below)

3 cups freshly squeezed lemon juice

$2\frac{1}{2}$ cups cold water

2 lemons, thinly sliced

Ice to fill two large pitchers

FOR LEMONADE

Combine simple syrup with lemon juice. Add $2\frac{1}{2}$ cups cold water, $\frac{1}{2}$ cup at a time, to reach desired sweetness level, keeping in mind that the ice in the pitcher will further dilute lemonade. Pour lemonade into pitcher of ice. Garnish with slices of lemon.

FOR SIMPLE SYRUP

Pour 6 cups water and $4\frac{1}{2}$ cups sugar into a deep saucepan and stir to combine. Warm over medium heat just until sugar is dissolved. Remove from heat and cool.

GOAT CHEESE AND WATERCRESS SANDWICHES

$\frac{1}{2}$ cup chopped watercress leaves

2 $5\frac{1}{2}$-ounce logs soft, fresh goat cheese (such as Montrachet), at room temperature

Kosher salt

16 thin slices sourdough or whole wheat sandwich bread, crusts removed

5 tablespoons unsalted butter, at room temperature

$\frac{3}{4}$ cup toasted walnuts, finely chopped

Watercress sprigs (to garnish platter)

1. In a medium bowl, fold chopped watercress leaves into goat cheese. Season to taste with salt. Spread mixture evenly over eight slices of bread. Top with remaining eight slices. Butter edges of sandwiches. Cut diagonally in half to make sixteen triangles.

2. Place walnuts on a plate. Dip buttered edges of sandwiches into nuts. Arrange sandwiches on a platter. Garnish with watercress sprigs.

Sandwiches can be made up to four hours ahead. Cover with plastic wrap and chill.

Makes 16 triangular half sandwiches

DEVILED CRAB SALAD SANDWICHES

1 pound jumbo lump crabmeat (about 2 cups)

1 cup mayonnaise

2 teaspoons Old Bay seasoning

2 teaspoons Dijon mustard

$1/4$ cup thinly sliced scallions

$1/4$ cup thinly sliced celery

12 thin slices pumpernickel bread (about $3 1/2$ inches square and $1/8$ inch thick)

8 tablespoons softened butter

$1/4$ cup thinly sliced red onion

4 hard-boiled eggs, thinly sliced

2–3 heads of crisp baby lettuce

1. In a medium-sized bowl combine the crab, mayonnaise, Old Bay seasoning, mustard, scallions, and celery. Mix gently until ingredients are evenly distributed and well coated with mayonnaise.

2. Place four slices of bread on a clean surface and spread a half tablespoon of butter on each slice. Spread each slice with one sixth of the crab salad and top with thin layers of onion, egg, and baby lettuce.

3. Butter both sides of four more slices of bread and top each half sandwich with one of these slices. Spread each sandwich with a third of the remaining deviled crab and the remaining onion, egg, and lettuce.

4. Close the sandwiches with the four remaining bread slices, spread on one side with the rest of the butter. Press firmly, butter side down, to "seal" the sandwich.

5. Slice off crusts then slice each sandwich into four triangular finger sandwiches and place on a platter.

6. Cover sandwiches with damp paper towel and plastic wrap, and chill for at least 30 minutes. (Crab salad may be made up to one day ahead and the assembled sandwiches up to several hours ahead.)

Makes 16 triangular three-layer tea sandwiches

TURKEY, BRIE, AND CHUTNEY SANDWICHES

16 slices thin whole-grain bread

1 jar good-quality, store-bought chutney (such as
   Major Grey's)

8 ounces turkey breast, thinly sliced

3 ounces Brie, thinly sliced

8 butter or Bibb lettuce leaves

1. Spread each slice of bread with enough chutney to cover one side.

2. Top half of the slices with turkey, Brie, and lettuce. Place the remaining eight slices of bread, chutney side down, on top of each sandwich.

3. Slice each sandwich into quarters and arrange on a platter to serve. (Sandwiches may be assembled up to 4 hours in advance, covered with plastic wrap, and refrigerated.)

Makes 24 square tea sandwiches

COCONUT CUPCAKES WITH WHITE CHOCOLATE FROSTING

CUPCAKES

$\frac{1}{2}$ cup coconut cream (not cream of coconut) or
   milk

3 large egg whites

$\frac{1}{2}$ teaspoon pure vanilla extract

$1\frac{1}{2}$ cups cake flour

2 teaspoons baking powder

6 tablespoons (3 ounces) unsalted butter, softened

$\frac{1}{2}$ teaspoon salt

$\frac{3}{4}$ cup granulated sugar

$\frac{1}{2}$ cup desiccated or unsweetened coconut, finely
   ground in a food processor

$\frac{1}{2}$ cup sweetened dried coconut

WHITE CHOCOLATE FROSTING

6 ounces white chocolate, finely chopped

$1\frac{3}{4}$ cups powdered sugar

$\frac{1}{4}$ cup milk

butter

$\frac{1}{2}$ teaspoon pure vanilla extract

$\frac{1}{4}$ teaspoon salt

TO MAKE THE CAKE

1. Preheat oven to 350°F. and set oven rack in the middle position. Lightly coat the surface of a twelve-cup cupcake pan with a nonstick spray and line each cup with a foil or paper liner.

2. In a small bowl, whisk together the coconut cream, egg whites, and vanilla extract to combine. In another bowl, or over parchment paper, sift together the flour and baking powder.

3. Beat the butter and salt together in an electric mixer fitted with a whisk until creamy and smooth and while continuing to beat add sugar in a steady stream. Beat on medium speed until light and fluffy, 2–3 minutes, stopping to scrape down the sides of the bowl as necessary.

4. Add one-third of the dry ingredients along with one-third of the coconut cream mixture and beat on low speed until just combined. Add the remaining dry ingredients and co-conut cream mixture in two alternating batches, beating between each addition to fully incorporate. Add the dried, ground coconut and sweetened dried coconut with the last addition of dry ingredients. Scrape down the bowl and give a final stir with a sturdy rubber spatula.

5. Fill each cupcake cup about two-thirds full and knock the pan on the countertop once or twice to release air bubbles and even the surface of the batter. Place pan in oven. After 10–12 minutes, rotate the pan 180 degrees and continue to bake until cake springs back when lightly pressed in the center and a cake tester or wooden skewer emerges with crumbs clinging to it. Total baking time will be 20–22 minutes.

6. Cool pan on a cooling rack for 5 minutes, then remove the cupcakes from the pan to the rack and let cool completely.

TO MAKE THE FROSTING

1. Melt white chocolate in a bowl set over a saucepan of water that is not quite simmering. Make sure the bottom of the bowl rests several inches above the surface of the water. Stir chocolate until smooth and let cool to room temperature on the countertop.

2. Sift the powdered sugar into a medium-sized bowl. Using a whisk, stir in the milk until all of the sugar has dissolved and mixture is smooth. Add butter, vanilla extract, and salt and continue to beat until smooth and shiny. With a rubber spatula, stir in the cooled white chocolate.

3. Place frosting in the refrigerator until cool enough to frost the cupcakes, about 30 minutes. (Frosting can be kept for a day in the refrigerator or at room temperature. Refrigerated frosting will need to soften at room temperature before spreading.)

Makes 12 cupcakes

CASUAL SUPPER

Who: Six close friends

When: Saturday at 6.30 P.M.

Where: Kitchen

What I'm wearing: Cashmere sweater and jeans

Soundtrack: Mellow but interesting, like George
   Winston piano

Favor: Softly scented sachets

This supper was a casual meal for friends; we ate in the kitchen and, for the entrée, everyone served herself from the carved chicken set out on the island. It was less work for the hostess than a formal sit-down in the dining room. This is the type of dinner I could easily host once a month, whereas the Little Black Dress dinner is a once or twice a year affair. If I were hosting a meal like this once a month, I might not go as over the top as I did here with the details but I do love making creative invitations, witty centerpieces, and heartfelt favors. This meal would taste just as good with a phone call to round up friends and a plain pillar candle glowing in the center of the table; I just wanted to show how you can embellish an easy menu and create a truly memorable night.

Roast chicken is one of my favorite dishes; it is so easygoing and there are many variations. As long as I carefully schedule when it needs to go into the oven and note that on my timeline, it takes care of itself once it's roasting—and who doesn't love arriving for dinner to find the aroma of roast chicken wafting through the house?

Olive oil

1 medium onion, chopped

1 cup peeled and diced eggplant

$1/4$ teaspoon chili pepper

Kosher salt and freshly ground black pepper

5 cloves garlic, minced

1 19-ounce can of cannellini beans, rinsed and
  drained

4 or 5 whole, peeled canned tomatoes, preferably
  Italian, coarsely chopped and juices reserved

4 portobello mushrooms, cleaned, stemmed, and
  sliced $1/4$-inch thick

1 medium-sized loaf country Italian bread, cut into
  12–14 thin slices and toasted

$1/2$ cup pesto

12–14 slices mozzarella cheese

Fresh basil to garnish

1. Preheat oven to 450°F. Line a baking sheet with foil.

2. Over medium heat, in a large sauté pan, sauté onion in olive oil until tender, 5–6 minutes. Add eggplant, chili pepper, several large pinches of salt, and 1–2 tablespoons more oil. Cook over medium-high heat, stirring frequently, until eggplant is golden brown and tender, about 2 minutes. Lower heat to medium, add garlic and continue to sauté for several minutes more. Stir in beans and chopped tomatoes and their juice. Remove from heat and set aside. (Eggplant-bean topping may be tightly sealed and stored in the refrigerator for 2 days before assembling the bruschetta.)

3. Toss mushroom slices in oil and sprinkle generously with salt and pepper. Place slices on prepared baking sheet and place in the oven. Roast until soft and fully cooked, 4 or 5 minutes.

4. To assemble bruschetta, spread each slice of toasted bread with pesto. Divide roasted portobello slices among bruschetta and spoon bean-and-eggplant mixture over the mushrooms. Top each with a slice of mozzarella. Place bruschetta on a baking sheet lined with foil or parchment paper.

5. Adjust oven rack to the highest position and turn oven to broil. Place baking sheet in the oven and broil just until cheese bubbles and browns and bean mixture is heated through, about one minute.

6. Garnish bruschetta with fresh basil leaves and serve.

Serves 6 to 8

PEAR AND BLUE CHEESE SALAD

VINAIGRETTE

1 shallot, minced

1 tablespoon Dijon mustard

2 tablespoons red wine vinegar

2 tablespoons honey

$\frac{1}{2}$ cup extra-virgin olive oil

Kosher salt and freshly ground black pepper to taste

SALAD

2 heads Bibb, Boston, or red-leaf lettuce, or a mixture

2 medium-sized ripe pears, peeled and sliced just before salad is dressed

$\frac{1}{3}$–$\frac{1}{2}$ cup blue cheese, crumbled

$\frac{1}{3}$–$\frac{1}{2}$ cup honey-roasted almonds, coarsely chopped

1. In a food processor fitted with the metal blade, pulse the shallot, mustard, red wine vinegar, and honey. With processor running, drizzle in olive oil. Stop processor when vinaigrette is smooth and emulsified. If it is too thick, add water, a few teaspoons at a time, and pulse to incorporate. Season to taste with salt and freshly ground pepper. (Keep in mind that the blue cheese in the salad will be quite salty on its own.)

2. In a large bowl, combine lettuce, pears, and blue cheese. Drizzle in several large spoonfuls of vinaigrette, pouring it around the sides of the bowl in circular motions. Gently and evenly coat the salad in the dressing, adding more as necessary. (Reserve remaining vinaigrette in the refrigerator for future use.)

3. Garnish with almonds.

Serves 6

ROAST CHICKEN

BRINE

16 cups water

1 cup granulated sugar

2 cups kosher salt

CHICKEN

2   4- to 5-pound roasting chickens, packages of innards removed

12 tablespoons (1$\frac{1}{2}$ sticks) unsalted butter, at room temperature

$\frac{1}{4}$ cup fresh parsley, coarsely chopped, plus 6 whole sprigs

$\frac{1}{4}$ cup fresh thyme, coarsely chopped, plus 6 whole sprigs

2 tablespoons fresh rosemary, coarsely chopped, plus 4 whole sprigs

1 tablespoon fennel seeds, crushed in a mortar and pestle or pulsed in a spice grinder

Olive oil for rubbing chickens

Freshly ground black pepper

3 medium onions, peeled and quartered

2 heads of garlic, cloves peeled

SAUCE

$1\frac{1}{2}$ cups chicken broth

$\frac{3}{4}$ cup dry white wine

1–2 tablespoons all-purpose flour

BRINE CHICKEN

1. Trim chickens of excess fat around the neck and tail ends of their main cavities.

2. In a tall stockpot, deep plastic tub, or clean bucket purchased for kitchen use, mix 6 cups water, sugar, and salt until crystals have dissolved. Place chickens in the brine and weigh down, if necessary, with a piece of parchment paper and an upside-down plate or two. Chickens should be completely submerged in the brine. Make more brine, if required by the dimensions of your pot or tub, using 4 cups water to $\frac{1}{2}$ cup salt to $\frac{1}{4}$ cup sugar.

3. Allow chickens to brine in the refrigerator for at least 1 to 2 hours or, at most, overnight. Then remove from brine, rinse briefly under cold water, and pat dry. Place on a foil-covered sheet pan and return to the refrigerator, uncovered, for a few more hours, or as long as a day, before preparing them to roast. (The longer their skin is exposed to the dry air of the refrigerator, the crispier and browner their skin will become during roasting.)

PREPARING HERB MIXTURE AND SEASONING CHICKENS

1. Preheat oven to 450°F.

2. Mix softened butter, chopped herbs, and crushed fennel seeds in a bowl. Reserve 2 tablespoons of the herb butter for the sauce.

3. Sprinkle cavities of chickens with freshly ground pepper and stuff with reserved whole sprigs of parsley, thyme, and rosemary.

4. Slide fingers between the skin and flesh of the breasts, and working your way down to the legs, gently pull skin away from flesh, creating space for herb butter. Take care not to tear the skin, as herb butter will leak out during roasting.

5. Divide the herb butter between the two chickens and spread it as evenly as possible under the skin from leg to breast. Tie chicken legs together with kitchen twine and tuck the smallest wing joints behind the preceding joint.

Place the chickens on their backs in a shallow, heavy-bottomed roasting pan and rub with olive oil from front to back so that chickens are well greased. Grind some pepper over their breasts and legs.

6. Place the roasting pan in the middle of the oven and roast for 30 minutes. In a bowl, toss the onion quarters and garlic cloves with enough olive oil to generously coat and season with salt and pepper. Scatter the onion and garlic around the chickens in the roasting pan and lower oven heat to 400°F. Continue to roast until the juices from the thickest part of the breasts and thighs run clear, stirring the onions and garlic occasionally so that they brown thoroughly. Remove roasting pan from oven, tilt chickens so that their juices run back into the pan, and place them on a carving board. Using a slotted spoon, remove onions and garlic to a plate and tent loosely with foil.

PREPARING THE SAUCE

1. Drain the rendered fat and oil from the roasting pan and place it over medium-high heat. Pour in the chicken broth and wine, scraping up any bits clinging to the bottom. Let the liquid reduce at a boil for a few minutes.

2. Transfer liquid to a saucepan and bring to a simmer. Meanwhile, mix reserved herb butter and flour together to form a paste that is the consistency of Play-Doh. Add the paste a knob at a time to the simmering liquid, whisking frequently, using only as much paste as is necessary to create a thickened sauce. Season with salt and a few grinds of pepper.

SEASONED POTATOES

$1/3$ cup kosher salt

5 medium-sized garlic cloves

2 teaspoons paprika

2 teaspoons chili powder

1 teaspoon turmeric

1 teaspoon poultry seasoning

1 teaspoon freshly ground white pepper

$1/2$ teaspoon ground ginger

$1/2$ teaspoon dried mustard

$1/2$ teaspoon celery seed

$1/2$ teaspoon onion powder

$1/2$ teaspoon dried dill weed

3 russet potatoes, scrubbed

Olive oil

1. Preheat oven to 400°F.

2. Place salt in a food processor fitted with the metal blade. With machine running, add garlic cloves and process until well minced, about 20 seconds. Transfer garlic salt to a bowl and stir in remaining seasonings.

3. Slice potatoes $1/4$-inch thick and arrange on two rimmed baking sheets lined with parchment paper or foil. Brush both sides of potato slices with olive oil. Sprinkle spice blend on the exposed side of each slice. Bake until both sides are golden, flipping slices once with a metal spatula after tops have colored, about 15 minutes through cooking.

Serves 6

RUSTIC PLUM TART

This delicious tart can be made with a variety of fruits; if you can't find plums, substitute 8–10 apricots or a pint of raspberries, blackberries, or blueberries.

PASTRY FOR NINE-INCH TART

1½ cups unbleached, all-purpose flour

1 tablespoon granulated sugar

½ teaspoon kosher salt

8 tablespoons (1 stick) unsalted butter, cubed and
     well chilled

FILLING

7-ounce tube of marzipan (sweetened almond paste)

8 plums, pitted and sliced into 6 wedges per plum

2 tablespoons melted butter

Granulated sugar for sprinkling on fruit

Powdered sugar for garnish

Premium vanilla ice cream for serving

1. Pulse flour, sugar, and salt together in the bowl of a food processor fitted with the metal blade. Add the butter to the dry ingredients and pulse until the pieces of butter are pea-sized. With the processor running, drizzle in ice water (up to ¼ cup) until the dough forms small balls that stick together when pressed. (You may need slightly less or slightly more ice water than is called for. If the dough appears dry and resists sticking together add more water, a splash at a time, until it comes together.)

2. Turn out contents of bowl onto a clean work surface and gather dough into a ball. Press down firmly to form a flat disc. Wrap snuggly in plastic wrap and allow to rest in the refrigerator for at least 1 hour and up to 24 hours.

3. Roll out the dough into an 11-inch circle; it will be about ⅛-inch thick.

4. Coax the circle of dough into the tart pan by letting it first slump into the pan before pressing it into the corners and up the sides. Roll the rolling pin firmly across the top of the tart pan to trim off excess dough. Place pan in the refrigerator to chill for 15 minutes.

5. Preheat the oven to 400°F.

6. Unwrap marzipan and roll it into a ball. On a lightly floured surface, roll ball into a 9-inch circle and transfer it to the tart pan, laying it on top of the pastry. Press marzipan into the base of the pan. Place sliced plums in a circular pattern on top of the marzipan, pressing each wedge into the marzipan to firmly anchor the fruit. Brush the melted butter over the top of the tart and if it is not especially sweet, sprinkle fruit with sugar.

7. Place tart pan on a parchment- or foil-lined baking sheet and transfer to a rack in the lowest part of the oven. Bake until crust has browned and fruit is soft and juicy. If the edges of tart are browning too quickly, shield the crust with foil.

8. Remove tart from the oven and allow to cool completely before unmolding and slicing. Sieve powdered sugar on top of each slice and serve with a scoop of vanilla ice cream.

Serves 6

RESOURCES

There are several stores that I frequent to help build my entertaining arsenal. Some of my favorites are listed below.

ANTHROPOLOGIE
800-309-2500
www.anthropologie.com

This home and clothing store offers an eclectic mix of thrift store finds and elegant serve ware. I love Anthropologie because it encourages mixing and matching. Many of their pieces are neutral in color and design, so they are very versatile.

BALLARD DESIGNS
800-536-7551
www.ballarddesigns.com

Ballard Designs specializes in European-inspired décor for the home. Carrying both furniture and accessories, it creates products like those found in European flea markets and couples them with current design trends. I particularly like to shop this store for unusual table décor, party elements, and extra seating when I entertain. If your style is French country, or even if it's not, you will inevitably find something perfect for your party here.

CALYX & COROLLA
800-800-7788
www.calyxandcorolla.com

When buying flowers for myself, I usually just pick them up from the local florist, but when sending them as a hostess gift, nobody delivers better than Calyx & Corolla. Its flowers always arrive fresh and with detailed care instructions that keep them lasting longer than your average mail-order bouquets.

COST PLUS WORLD MARKET
800-COST-PLUS
www.costplusmarket.com

This store is fantastic for inexpensive ethnic finds. Not only does it have an amazing selection of ethnic cookware and serve ware, it also has a food section that carries many hard-to-find spices and regional ingredients.

CRANE & CO.
800-268-2281
www.crane.com

This is a wonderful stationery store for special-occasion stationery that needs to look especially refined. Its paper can be pricey but check online in its clearance section for cheaper alternatives.

CRATE AND BARREL
800-996-9960
www.crateandbarrel.com

Crate and Barrel is a wonderful spot to buy neutral pieces for your entertaining arsenal as well as festive additions. It has a particularly vast selection of glassware. It carries a wide range of styles, and its price point is reasonable. It rarely discontinues a glass pattern, which is convenient when one breaks and needs to be replaced!

HARNEY & SONS FINE TEAS
888-427-6398
www.harney.com

This website provides a large variety of teas and important taste information. Harney offers teas that are hard to find anywhere else, including wedding and kosher teas. It also offers expert advice about brewing the perfect pot of tea.

JO ANN'S
800-525-4951
www.joann.com

Jo Ann's and Jo Ann's Etc. stores are a crafter's paradise. Name a craft and it sells the materials to do it. I shop Jo Ann's, in particular, for rubber stamping, invitation, and artificial floral needs. In addition to the craft section, the expanded stores carry home-decorator fabric and sewing notions, which are great for making your own tablecloths and napkins.

KATE'S PAPERIE
800-809-9880
www.katespaperie.com

This store in New York is a real treat. It used to be available only to lucky New Yorkers; now you (and I) can visit and shop it on the web.

It has a beautiful selection of papers, ribbons, and crafting items specifically for paper crafts and invitations. This is definitely my favorite paper store, and every time I am in New York I spend some quality time here.

MICHAELS CRAFT STORE
800-Michaels
www.michaels.com

Michaels carries all things related to crafts. Anything you need to help create that unique centerpiece or clever favors is available here. It has an extensive bead and embellishment section as well as invitation materials. For gifts and favors, I buy its inexpensive plain picture frames and decorate them myself with supplies found around the store.

NICHOLAS KNIEL
404-252-8855
www.nicholaskniel.com

Because I adore using ribbons in most of my projects, I am in this store at least twice a week. Designer-owned, Nicholas Kniel carries the very best in new and vintage ribbon, buttons, feathers, and millinery flowers. Everything in this store is handpicked by Nicholas himself. While not exactly inexpensive, this shop carries only the crème de la crème of ribbons and embellishments. If you are looking for something truly unique and unsurpassed in quality, this is the store for you.

OFFRAY RIBBON
800-237-9425
www.offray.com

One of the largest manufacturers in the country, Offray offers the widest selection of ribbon. It carries all types of ribbon: wired, un-wired, seasonal, plaids, metallics, and prints. It offers the largest color options in grosgrain and double-faced satin ribbon. Its products are available nationwide at craft stores such as Jo Ann's and Michaels. I specifically enjoy its vast color selection of grosgrains and use them frequently when wrapping gifts or working with paper crafts.

PIER I IMPORTS
800-295-4595
www.pier1.com

Much like Cost Plus World Market, Pier 1 offers unique and colorful entertaining items. It has a nice selection of ethnic serve ware as well as traditional selections. It also has a nice candle section with unique display options.

POTTERY BARN
800-922-5507
www.potterybarn.com

While Pottery Barn does carry plates and glasses, I love this store for its seasonal and music CDs. When it comes to entertaining, it always has a changing supply of tabletop additions such as place-mats, napkin rings, place-card holders, and other accessories. If you are looking for good party music, peruse Pottery Barn's selections. It has great mix CDs with upbeat music that is mellow enough for entertaining needs.

SMITH AND HAWKEN
800-776-3336
www.smithandhawken.com

Whenever I am doing a party outside or incorporating gardening elements into my party, this is the shop I go to. It carries beautiful urns and other pots for planting, which I use frequently for center-pieces. It also has interesting decorations during the holiday season. Although not exactly inexpensive, everything in this store is extremely tasteful and beautiful.

STAPLES
800-208-3Staple
www.staples.com

Staples is a wonderful place to pick up a corkboard for your inspiration board, or notebooks, binders, and folders for your style file. You can also find a huge variety of mailing labels and envelopes at reasonable prices.

SUR LA TABLE
800-243-0852
www.surlatable.com

I felt I had died and gone to heaven when I found this culinary delight! Everything the home chef needs and more can be found at this store. It carries kitchen equipment, plates, accessories—basically, if it has to do with preparing food, it probably carries it.

TARGET

800-591-3869

www.target.com

Without question, my favorite store on the planet. Target has an amazing selection of everything from candles to serve ware, to linens, to home accessories, to seasonal items, particularly some of the most elegant pieces for very little money. Over the years, I have accessorized my home predominantly from this discount store. Target hits the bull's-eye with me because it continues to sell unique and stylish items all at a price I can afford.

WEST ELM

866-WESTELM

www.westelm.com

Although this isn't the style I normally go for, West Elm has really wonderful modern but comfortable pieces, and it doesn't hurt that it has a real knack for stylish pieces without heart-stopping price tags.

WILLIAMS-SONOMA

877-812-6235

www.williams-sonoma.com

A playground for cooks, Williams-Sonoma offers beautiful place settings, linens, glassware, and all the extras that make a table setting beautiful. It also has everything you need to prepare the food. I particularly enjoy its small grocery section that offers ready-made marinades and sauces as well as baking mixes. All around, this is one of my favorite shops.

YVES DELORME

800-322-3911

www.yvesdelorme.com

Everything in this store is beautiful to look at and touch. Carrying only the best in quality, Yves Delorme's distinctive table linens turn a table from ordinary to extraordinary. From pure white linen for formal entertaining to colorful printed cotton for breakfast on the porch, its tablecloths, napkins, and placemats make every meal special.

MY FAVORITES AROUND ATLANTA

404-233-3400

BOXWOOD GARDENS AND GIFTS, INC.

This Atlanta store has it all, from tabletop and home décor to unique gifts and garden items. I enjoy this shop for its floral department. The selection of potted plants and flowers is amazing, and its floral department puts together some of the most beautiful arrangements I have ever seen.

THE GRAPE

678-309-9463

www.yourgrape.com

A wine-tasting bar and store, this shop carries unique and reasonably priced wines. It's a great place to experiment and expand your wine knowledge as you can taste any wine before purchasing a bottle. I love shopping for wine here because the staff is knowledgeable and their attitude is refreshingly just right. Their motto reads: "Lables are not important, taste is all that counts." I could not have said it better myself!

LUSH LIFE GARDEN AND FLOWERS

404-841-9661

Many of the flowers featured in this book came from this Atlanta store. In addition to freshly cut flowers, Lush Life carries a beautiful assortment of things for the home and garden. If you are looking for something unique to dress the table for your next dinner party, take a peek at what it has in store.

MUSS & TURNER'S

770-434-1114

www.mussandturners.com

Whenever I am hosting a party, I visit this gourmet market for its exceptional quality food, wine, and personal service. In addition to prepared foods, Muss & Turner's offers the most amazing and unique selection of cheeses, meats, and accompaniments. Serving only the highest quality products and owned and operated by two of the kindest guys on the planet, this store is a real treat to visit.

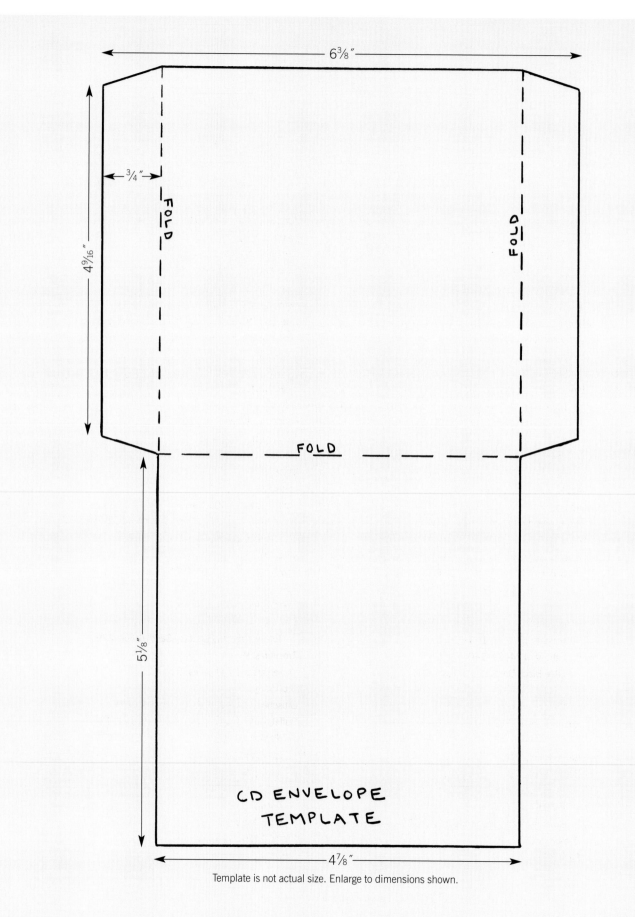

6 3/8"

3/4"

4 9/16"

FOLD

FOLD

FOLD

5 1/8"

CD ENVELOPE
TEMPLATE

4 7/8"

Template is not actual size. Enlarge to dimensions shown.

INDEX